POLITICS

HACKS

**100 clever ways to help you understand
and remember the most important theories**

JULIAN FLANDERS

CASSELL
ILLUSTRATED

For Cathy, Polly and George

An Hachette UK Company
www.hachette.co.uk

First published in Great Britain in 2018 by Cassell,
an imprint of Octopus Publishing Group Ltd
Carmelite House
50 Victoria Embankment
London EC4Y 0DZ
www.octopusbooks.co.uk

Distributed in the US by
Hachette Book Group
1290 Avenue of the Americas
4th and 5th Floors
New York, NY 10104

Distributed in Canada by
Canadian Manda Group
664 Annette St.
Toronto, Ontario, Canada M6S 2C8

ISBN 978-1-78840-040-4

A CIP catalogue record for this book is available from the British Library.

Printed and bound in China

10 9 8 7 6 5 4 3 2 1

Publishing Director: Trevor Davies
Senior Editor: Alex Stetter
Junior Designer: Jack Storey
Design and layout: Simon Buchanan, Design 23
Illustrators: Design 23
Copy editor: Linda Schofield
Indexer: Isobel McLean
Senior Production Manager: Peter Hunt

Contents

Introduction

We all know what politics means, don't we? Or do we? It is governance, it is how we should live, it is who should get what, it is how much tax we should pay. The fact is that politics is essential to almost every aspect of our lives. In 1946, George Orwell asserted that, "In our age there is no such thing as 'keeping out of politics'. All issues are political issues..." He was right then and, of course, he would be right today. It seems a shame then – actually, it is a scandal – when you overhear people say, "I don't like politics", or even worse, "I don't understand politics". Both statements are unacceptable.

However complicated politics may be, understanding it is a responsibility that we should all be prepared to take. Of course, politics has existed for a long time – since humans first organized themselves into communities in Asia sometime around 9000 BCE – and so can appear too vast and complicated a subject to comprehend. And there has also been a lot of it over the years, in newspapers, magazines, radio, television, film, advertising and websites. Of course, it has gone through peaks and troughs of interest, often because of the politicians involved, over the years this has included Cicero, Thomas Aquinas, Mary Wollstonecraft, George Washington, Lenin, Mao Zedong, Franklin D. Roosevelt, Winston Churchill, Barack Obama and Donald Trump, heroes to some, villains to others depending on where you stand on the political spectrum, of course.

Whether you like it or not, politics has always been big news. We cannot and should not ignore it. The information is all there, but, as much of the news we consume is politically biased and aimed at trying to persuade us to adopt certain views, we must educate ourselves so that we can read between the lines. That is where *Politics Hacks* comes in.

This book takes 100 political themes or concepts and explains them in bite-sized chunks. They might be historical political documents or events, such as the Communist Manifesto or the French Revolution; they might be ideologies or systems of government, like conservativism or anarchy; they might concern economics, law or science and the environment. Taken together and explained in detail and in context, they will provide a window through which you can begin to understand the intricacies of more than 5000 years of political machinations. Even if you do not like politics because, as Orwell went on to say, it is "a mass of lies, evasions, folly, hatred and schizophrenia", it is your duty as a citizen to understand it, take up a position and vote accordingly. *Politics Hacks* is here to help you on your way.

No.1

The Birth of Power Politics

Hatshepsut's unprecedented power

Hatshepsut // c.1507–c.1458 BCE

 1/ Helicopter View: Though she cannot claim to be the first female political leader in history, Hatshepsut (c.1507–c.1458 BCE) is rightly regarded as one of the most successful. Despite facing innumerable obstacles, she became pharaoh of the richest and most powerful state in the ancient world in 1478 BCE. Having seized power, she used her political skills to maintain her leadership for over 20 years. Born of a royal bloodline as the eldest daughter of Thutmose I and Queen Ahmose, Hatshepsut married her younger half-brother, Thutmose II, whose untimely death left her, aged 16, acting as queen and co-regent for Thutmose III, his son by another wife, who was three years old. This was not unusual in Egypt, but as a woman she was expected to stand aside when he came of age. However, and no one really knows why, after seven years of conventional co-regency, she was crowned pharaoh. Of course, the move was met with objections and, given her precarious position both as a woman and because of the presence of a male heir, she set out to demonstrate her authority as the legitimate ruler.

Reliefs at Hatshepsut's temple at Dayr al-Baḥrī in the Valley of the Kings, Egypt depict her successful trade expedition to Punt.

2/Shortcut: Making full use of the mechanisms of propaganda, Hatshepsut "changed" her gender, wearing men's clothes and sporting a beard in many depictions to allay the fears of those who did not want a female pharaoh, embarked on extensive building projects and also changed her birth story, claiming that her father was Amun-Re, Egypt's chief deity. But the best example of her political nous was in mounting an expedition to Punt (thought to be in present-day Somalia or Eritrea), one of Egypt's traditional trading allies with whom trade had stopped some 500 years before. Five ships made the trip down the Nile to the Red Sea and on to Punt, carrying jewellery, tools and weapons. They returned with gold, ebony, wild animals, animal skins, ivory, spices, precious woods, cosmetics, incense and myrrh trees. The expedition was a political and financial triumph, reopening a lucrative trade route and helping Hatshepsut in other significant ways: it kept the army busy so preventing possible insurrection, underlined to the ancient world the strength of Egypt and, most importantly, legitimized Hatshepsut's position as "king".

3/Hack: Hatshepsut was the first leader to show the value of political manipulation.

No.2
A "Good" Society
Confucius's government by example

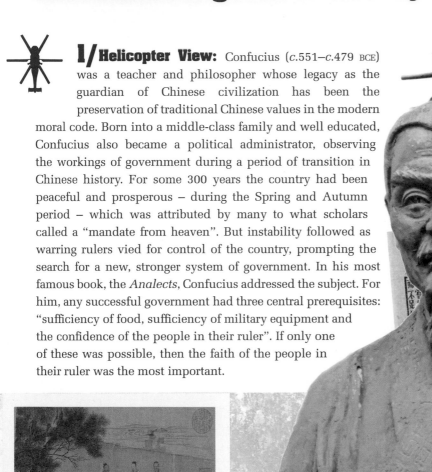

1/Helicopter View: Confucius (*c.*551–*c.*479 BCE) was a teacher and philosopher whose legacy as the guardian of Chinese civilization has been the preservation of traditional Chinese values in the modern moral code. Born into a middle-class family and well educated, Confucius also became a political administrator, observing the workings of government during a period of transition in Chinese history. For some 300 years the country had been peaceful and prosperous – during the Spring and Autumn period – which was attributed by many to what scholars called a "mandate from heaven". But instability followed as warring rulers vied for control of the country, prompting the search for a new, stronger system of government. In his most famous book, the *Analects*, Confucius addressed the subject. For him, any successful government had three central prerequisites: "sufficiency of food, sufficiency of military equipment and the confidence of the people in their ruler". If only one of these was possible, then the faith of the people in their ruler was the most important.

Confucius // *c.*551–*c.*479 BCE

2/Shortcut: Confucius believed that in order to create a "good society", everything had to be in harmony, in its correct and natural place. Though he did not believe all men were born perfect, by pursuing the traditional Chinese virtues of duty, loyalty and respect each individual could, and indeed was duty bound to, become a *junzi*, a "superior man", whose character would act as an example to others. At the top of his imagined societal hierarchy sat the sovereign, who earned his place on merit, and whose role it was to lead by example and through self-discipline (in order to govern others, one first has to govern oneself), to treat the populace with compassion and win its affections and respect. Below him came the ministers, also of the highest moral character, who were also to lead by example and to advise both the sovereign and his subjects. In turn, the people, treated with respect and knowing their place in society, want to fulfil its needs to the best of their abilities. "If a leader's desire is for good," he wrote, "the people will be good."

Confucius's major work, the *Analects*, was published long after his death. Celebrations of his life take place in September each year in his birthplace in Qufu a city in Shandong Province.

See also //

3 The Art of War, p.10

3/Hack: Confucius believed that through self-discipline a leader should govern by example.

No.3
The Art of War
Politics and conflict

1/Helicopter View: Just as the end of the prosperous so-called Spring and Autumn period of late 6th-century China heralded new thinking on government, it also prompted a realization that the ability to make war was of vital importance in protecting the prosperity of the state, particularly during times of political instability. The first iteration of this came in the shape of *The Art of War*, a book traditionally attributed to Sun Tzu (*c*.554–*c*.496 BCE), a general in the army of the King of Wu. Ostensibly a guide to strategy and tactics for rulers and military commanders, it included advice on manoeuvres, communication, supplies, the use of terrain and of spies, the weather, and the treatment of soldiers and captives. However, its uniqueness lies in its exploration of new ideas on international relations, the business of war and the employment of military intelligence, which reveal the close relationship between politics and military policy, a notion that has influenced military strategists to this day.

Little is known about Sun Tzu, but many consider the book attributed to him to be the best ever written about war.

2/Shortcut: Sun Tzu examines the role of the army in protecting the state. He shares the idea with Confucius that moral leadership begins at the top, with the ruler leading by example, advised by his general and supported by the people. He emphasizes the significance of the quality of leadership and the need for the general to instill organization into his soldiers through training and discipline. His intentions are not aggressive, however, explaining how making alliances, collecting intelligence on your enemies, even deceiving them if necessary, are essential to avoid conflict. For him, a wise general will not fight unless he has to; after all, peace is less expensive. If you are forced to fight, though, it is important to think about the outcome of your actions, go for the hearts and minds of your enemies and fight for justice with appropriateness and moderation. These notions, particularly concerning conflict resolution, remain decidedly relevant in today's world. They are still used by the military but have also been adapted for business, sport and education.

See also //
2 A "Good" Society, p.8

3/Hack: This seminal work was the first to set out the relationship between war and the state.

No.4

Plato's *Republic*
The ideal state

Plato // 427–347 BCE

1/Helicopter View: In the 6th century BCE Athens was the centre of a well-to-do city-state with an educated population. In 510 BCE, the tyrant king Hippias was deposed and a new type of government was set up with political power given over to a popular assembly, which all eligible male citizens were urged to attend. One such person was Plato (427–347 BCE), a teacher and philosopher from a noble Athenian family. Given such an opportunity, Plato, and others, joined in serious discussions as to what sort of society the citizens would like to live in and how it would be governed and administered. Plato presented contemporary thinking in his book, the *Republic*. It takes the form of a dialogue between friends who want to outline a policy for the well-being of "just" citizens in a "just" state, as a model for any existing or emerging societies in the future. They discuss a range of subjects, including law, the carriage of justice, the education of ideal citizens and whether there is a place in the ideal state for the arts.

An illustration of the "Allegory of the Cave" by Jan Saenredam (1604) (opposite), a story Plato used to explain the role of the philosopher.

2/ Shortcut: Plato presents the state as a metaphor for the soul, with the people as its organs. As an organ cannot survive without a body, so an individual is nothing without the state. Of course, they both require balance to be happy and stable. Based on the concepts of justice and virtue, which would provide everyone with what is "due" to them, the state would be headed up by a "philosopher king", as philosophy is based on reason and is therefore the highest virtue. The populace would be composed of three separate classes: the ruling class, highly educated in philosophy, which would administer it; a military class, having courage and physical strength, which would defend it; and a professional class to be ruled and to deal with the ordinary daily affairs of the state. There was to be no intermingling between the classes. State education would be provided for all and there were to be equal rights for both sexes. In contrast to this apparent liberalism, Plato declared that the arts and literature would be banned to save the youth from moral degradation.

See also //
5 True Government, p.14

3/ Hack: Plato's *Republic* represents the first philosophical examination of the role of justice in society.

No.5
True Government
Aristotle's good life

Aristotle // 382–322 BCE

1/Helicopter View: One of Plato's students in Athens was a member of a royal family from the north-east of Greece named Aristotle (384–322 BCE). Aristotle's views of the world differed from those of his mentor. He felt that knowledge was acquired through observation rather than the intellect. He spent time studying animals and plants before turning his attention to the various systems of government that existed in Greece's city-states in order to determine which system was the most desirable. In order to do this, he posed two questions of each system: who rules and who do they rule for? Given that their "nature" leads humans to form social units — households, villages, cities, etc. — and that they all want to lead "good lives", he identified six types of government by their constitutional organization and labelled each as either "true" or "despotic".

2/ Shortcut: The "true" forms of government, monarchy, aristocracy and polity are those in which one, a few or many govern with a view to the common interest of everyone. The "despotic" systems – tyranny, oligarchy and democracy – are those in which wealth and power are created only for individuals or small groups. Each true form of government had its despotic twin. Thus, monarchy was good when the king or queen worked for the greater good. If the monarch ruled only to increase the monarchy's power then it would be tyrannical. Similarly, rule by an elite aristocracy was effective when the few worked for the good of all, but self-interest among that elite would set the rich against the poor in a corrupt oligarchy. Aristotle considered democracy as corrupt in that it could cause competition between the classes, although scholars argue that a democracy then differs from the modern-day model, which is in fact closer in character to his chosen model of polity, in which decisions are made on the basis of statutes rather than personal ideals or emotions. For Aristotle, this was the system that gave its citizens the best chance of a "good life".

Aristotle contributed to many aspects of human knowledge, from logic and biology to ethics and aesthetics, including his view of "true" and "despotic" forms of government.

See also //

4 Plato's *Republic*, p.12

	True	**Despotic**
One Ruler	Monarchy	Tyranny
Few Ruler	Aristocracy	Oligarchy
Many Rulers	Polity	Democracy

3/ Hack: Aristotle's observations served as a template for constitutional government.

No.6
Natural Law
Cicero's liberty

Cicero // 106–43 BCE

1/ Helicopter View: Marcus Tullius Cicero (106–43 BCE) was a high-ranking politician, philosopher, lawyer and orator whose life spanned the decline and fall of the Roman Republic and who played an important part in the significant political events of that time. The Republic, which lasted for almost 500 years, was a marvel of efficient and just government. It was ruled through a Senate, which made the laws, two annually elected Consuls, who performed executive duties, and a popular assembly. Heavily influenced by Plato and other Greek thinkers, Cicero was a great supporter of this constitution. But as the Republic grew strong and rich, its efficacy began to fail. It had become too large and the haves lost touch with the have-nots, resulting in civil wars and social strife. As Cicero watched these political convulsions he began to review his thinking on the principles of law on which it was founded. Following the Platonic tradition, he wrote his thoughts down in the form of a dialogue called *De Legibus* (*On the Laws*) (*c*.51 BCE).

Cicero used his considerable skills as an orator on many occasions, notably in 63 BCE, during a speech in the Senate when he exposed a plot led by Catiline to overthrow the Republic.

2/ Shortcut: Cicero foresaw the dangers posed by a tyrannical Consul. Although he believed that men were inherently good, he reasoned that as written laws might be made by tyrants – men corrupted by lust for pleasure, wealth and status – then they cannot be made by man. Cicero insisted that justice and law should derive their origins from God himself to ensure their eternal and immutable morality. He made a distinction between *legalism* (man-made law) and *natural law* (right and wrong as dictated by eternal wisdom). Cicero believed that human happiness is found in a life that accords with nature because human nature and the law of nature are ultimately the same thing. For him, natural law is a higher law and should therefore be the basis through which justice is dispensed. Cicero's fears were proved right in 44 BCE when the disgruntled Julius Caesar dissolved the Republic and declared himself dictator.

See also //
4 Plato's *Republic*, p.12

3/ Hack: Cicero's insights into the nature of liberty guided the development of law in Europe for centuries.

No.7
Feudalism The business of protection

1/ Helicopter View: Feudalism was a social and legal system that arose in Europe sometime in the Dark Ages, though historians have also identified its use in imperial Rome, Japan and China. It was regarded as an efficient economic system before the common use of money. It flourished during the 9th century in places without stable public authority, in which violence was common and protection against it often necessary. In theory, feudalism relied on the absolute power of the king, who owned all the land. Reserving much of the land for himself, the king would portion out the remainder to his nobles or lords, who, in turn, promised to fight for him. The lords rented out their land and offered protection to vassals, men they trusted, who controlled their portion of land and the people living on it. In return for protection, the vassals would pay "taxes" in the form of grain, vegetables and meat and provide military service when necessary. At the bottom of the pile were the peasants who worked the land and harvested its fruits. For them, life was hard; they had food, a place to sleep and some protection, in theory, but often not in practice.

Feudalism was the primary system of land distribution in medieval Europe.

2/Shortcut: Feudalism was brought to England by William the Conqueror, where it was formalized and written into the laws of the land. The system was particularly successful there because it was imposed on a society already used to royal prerogative. It brought order during a chaotic period, which allowed long-term progress in agricultural development. However, it deprived peasant families of land they had owned for generations, turning them into indentured servants and obliging them to give up a portion of their already scarce resources. The system was firmly established in Europe by the 14th century, though by this time abuse was rife, with injustice and lawlessness commonplace. Feudalism was brought down by the Black Death, which began in Asia sometime in the 1330s. By 1351 between 30 and 50 percent of the population of Europe had died, breaking the pyramid of power by decreasing the value of land and increasing the value of labour.

The pyramid of power that comprised the political, military and social system in the Middle Ages.

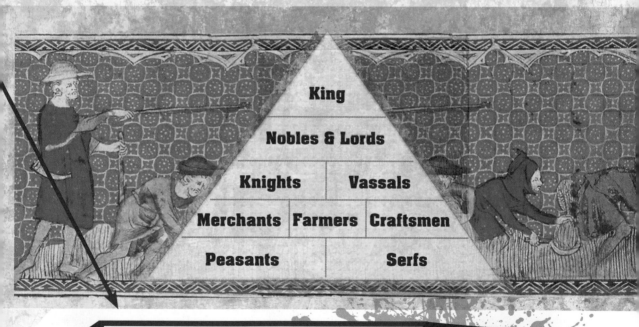

King

Nobles & Lords

Knights — Vassals

Merchants — Farmers — Craftsmen

Peasants — Serfs

3/Hack: Feudalism is a form of government based on the exchange of land for service.

No.8
The Just War Theory
Morality and conflict

1/Helicopter View: Though many great thinkers have added to the theory, the model of a "just war" is most often associated with the Italian scholar and priest Thomas Aquinas (1225–74). For Aquinas, war was one of the worst evils suffered by the human race. His theory was intended to motivate states to find ways of preventing war and limiting its consequences wherever possible. However, if conflict was inevitable, particularly for the protection of Christian values, then he stated that it had to conform to certain moralities. Aquinas's conditions of a just war are determined both by the reasons for starting it and its conduct when the fighting begins. Firstly, the war must be the last resort, undertaken only when diplomatic negotiations have failed. There must be just cause for conflict, rather for self-defence than for greed. It should be declared only by a legally recognized authority, e.g. a government or a king or queen. It must have the right intention: to fight evil or to establish good. It should be a war that is possible to win, using proportional force. No civilians should be involved and there should be no unnecessary cruelty.

St Thomas Aquinas // 1225–74

2/ Shortcut: Until the 20th century, history informs us that it was possible to fight a just war, as many churches supported their countries in "just" conflicts. The First World War (1914–18), however, with 18 million dead and 23 million wounded, failed to comply with a number of Aquinas's criteria, particularly its causes, its conduct and the treaty that ended it. In contrast, the Second World War (1939–45) appears to have met most of the conditions of a just war: negotiations with Hitler had failed and the Allied governments declared war on Germany for invading other countries. The Allies felt that they had a reasonable chance of success and intended to correct the evils of the Nazi regime. The majority of the fighting was limited to the armies concerned, and took place in harbours, munitions factories and on open ground. Some actions, however, such as the carpet bombing of cities like Dresden and London, killing hundreds of thousands of civilians, certainly broke the conditions.

According to Aquinas's theory, the First World War was unjust, due to its use of poison gas, while the Second World War was just, despite the merciless bombing of cities like London and Dresden.

See also //

9 Church and State, p.22

22 Age of Extremes, p.48

73 The Treaty of Versailles, p.150

3/ Hack: Aquinas's "just war" theory set out the parameters of a morally sound conflict.

No.9
Church and State
Chasing the people's loyalty

1/ Helicopter View: During the years of the Roman Empire and the Middle Ages, both spiritual and political thinking was dominated by the Church, a situation formalized in 800 when Charlemagne was crowned emperor of Rome and founded the Holy Roman Empire. By this time Christianity had been adopted as the official religion of Rome. The society supported by the Christian clergy was rigid, insisting on the primacy of divine spirituality and left little room for dissent. But as the Church's power grew, there was a decline in clerical standards resulting in its authority being called into question. During this time, in Asia and Africa another powerful religion began to emerge, Islam, and with it came a new wave of more secular political thinking. Christian thinkers – like Thomas Aquinas – influenced by these fresh ideas, began to re-examine age-old questions, like the divine right of kings and the primacy of divine law over secular law, a conflict that prompted a struggle between Church and state that ran right through the Middle Ages.

On Christmas morning, 800 AD, at St Peter's Basilica in Rome, Charlemagne was crowned emperor of Rome by Pope Leo III.

2/ Shortcut: As secular rulers began to contest for power in Europe there was a rise in nationalism and so conflicts between emperors and kings and the popes in Rome became inevitable. Aquinas and others, often referring back to Aristotle's thinking that a "good" society should be organized by reason, began to argue that it was not the Church's function to govern, but rather that effective government should be organized by the people who would elect their ruler, agree the legislation under which they lived and participate in the process of government. The power of the papacy was further eroded by internal arguments and the Great Schism of the late 1300s, when two or three rival popes were appointed at the same time. As a result of this, the prestige of the Church fell in all parts of Europe. As the Middle Ages drew to a close, people continued to challenge Church authority but also began to question the power of the monarch.

Between 1309 and 1376 the pope resided in Avignon. Pope Gregory XI returned to Rome in 1376, ending the Avignon Papacy, but his death in 1378 led to a split in the Catholic church over the choice of his successor.

See also //

5 True Government, p.14

3/ Hack: The separation of Church and state is a principle that underpins the foundation of democracy.

No.10
The Art of Leadership
Machiavelli's *The Prince*

1/Helicopter View: Born in the powerful city-state of Florence, Niccolò Machiavelli (1469–1527) lived in turbulent times. The Italian peninsula was rife with political conflict involving the major city-states of his home town, Milan, Venice and Naples as well as the papacy, France, Italy and the Holy Roman Empire. The son of a legal official, Machiavelli began a career in government just as the Medici family's 60-year rule in Renaissance Florence was coming to an end. Between 1499 and 1512 he undertook diplomatic missions up and down the Italian peninsula, also visiting the French, papal and Habsburg courts. He became well acquainted with the political tactics of the time as practised by Cesare Borgia, Pope Alexander VI, Louis XII and others. In 1512, the Medici were restored to power in Florence and Machiavelli, suspected of conspiring against them, was arrested. However, he was later released and retired to his country estate to write.

In *The Prince*, Machiavelli laid bare the moral world of politics and the gulf between conscience and the demands of public action.

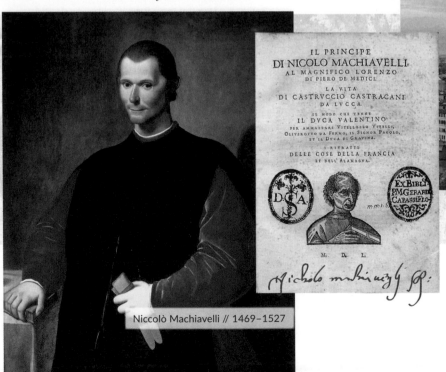

Niccolò Machiavelli // 1469–1527

2/ Shortcut: Machiavelli's most famous work, *The Prince*, was written in 1513, but not published until five years after his death. It was written as a practical guide on how to acquire power and keep it, based on the lessons of history and his own experiences as a diplomat. In it he counsels that rulers should not be guided by conventional ideas of virtue and morality and says that in order to maintain the well-being of the state – a ruler's principal aim – he "is often obliged to act against his promises, against charity, against humanity and against religion" because in politics the end always justifies the means no matter how immoral. Machiavelli's belief that politics had its own rules provoked huge controversy. The book was condemned by Pope Clement VIII and the word "Machiavellian" came to be used as a synonym for political manoeuvres marked by cunning, duplicity and bad faith. However, modern interpretations of this work are much kinder and *The Prince* is now credited with providing a warning to ensure that the structure of government creates good and just laws for the benefit of all citizens.

Cesare Borgia // 1475–1507

3/ Hack: *The Prince* proposes a system of government based on political realism rather than morality or higher law.

No.11
Man's State of Nature
Rule by social contract

Thomas Hobbes // 1588–1679

1/Helicopter View: The 18th century witnessed the ushering in of the Age of Enlightenment (or Reason) during which European thinkers began to question traditional religious doctrine and promote the idea that rational thought should be the primary source of authority in science, economics, law and politics. One such thinker was the English philosopher and teacher Thomas Hobbes (1588–1679), who was a strong advocate of Machiavelli's political realism in searching for stability in what was an unstable world. In seeking to justify a more practical approach to government, in his book, *Leviathan*, published in 1651, Hobbes sought to ask how the human race would behave if left ungoverned in a "state of nature". His conclusion, probably influenced by the bloody conflict of the English Civil War (1642–51) and the trial and execution of King Charles I in 1649, was that such a life would be one of "continual fear, and danger of violent death…nasty, brutish and short".

The execution of Charles I (opposite) during the English Civil War caused Thomas Hobbes to intensify his efforts to get his book *Leviathan* into print.

2/Shortcut: If left in a "state of nature", Hobbes suggested, humans would be driven toward self-gratification and self-protection and find themselves in a state of perpetual civil war. But, as humans were rational and could see that peace was good, they needed to be ruled by government, so how could they break away from this predicament? Based on the idea shared by a number of the political philosophers of the Enlightenment that citizens should be part of a "social contract" in which they give up some of their liberty by submitting to the authority of a third party and the rules of government in return for safety and the rule of law, Hobbes advocated for a "common-wealth" under an absolute monarch – or "Leviathan" – in order to prevent the collapse of social order. If the monarch failed in his or her duty, however, the social contract would be broken and the monarch replaced.

See also //
10 The Art of Leadership, p.24
14 A Civil Society, p.32
15 Power to the People, p.34

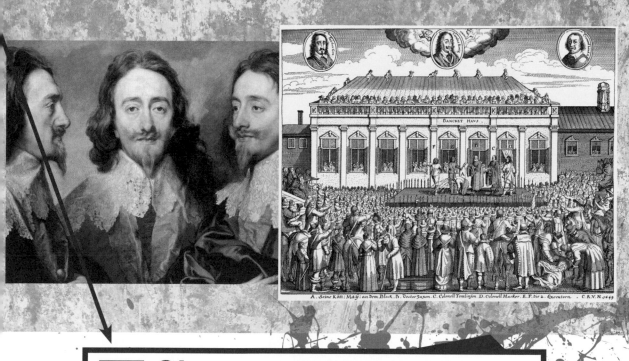

3/Hack: Hobbes's *Leviathan* posed the question: how can we divide power effectively between government and the people?

No.12
Money, Taxes and Commerce

David Hume's Enlightened thinking

David Hume // 1711–76

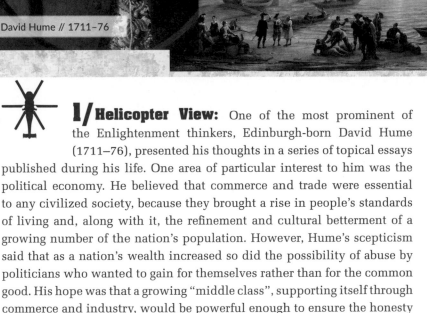

1/Helicopter View: One of the most prominent of the Enlightenment thinkers, Edinburgh-born David Hume (1711–76), presented his thoughts in a series of topical essays published during his life. One area of particular interest to him was the political economy. He believed that commerce and trade were essential to any civilized society, because they brought a rise in people's standards of living and, along with it, the refinement and cultural betterment of a growing number of the nation's population. However, Hume's scepticism said that as a nation's wealth increased so did the possibility of abuse by politicians who wanted to gain for themselves rather than for the common good. His hope was that a growing "middle class", supporting itself through commerce and industry, would be powerful enough to ensure the honesty of the state by checking any ambitions it might have to profit dishonestly through taxes or other tariffs.

2/Shortcut: Hume was particularly scathing on the subject of mercantilism, a policy practised by Britain and other European countries from the 16th to the 18th centuries, in which countries attempted to amass wealth through trade, exporting more than they imported and increasing stores of gold and precious metals. He pointed out that the amount of money in a society is of little importance; it is commodities that matter, and argued in favour of a free and open market, which would balance itself through self-regulation. He was a great advocate of international trade, noting that such commerce would widen the circle of goods and services a nation can have access to from countries possessing different resources and climates. Hume was a close friend of the economist Adam Smith (1723–90). According to Dennis C. Rasmussen, in his book, *The Infidel and the Professor* (2017), the two often discussed their work. It seems likely then that Hume was influential in Smith's arguments against mercantilism and in favour of free trade contained in his book, *The Wealth of Nations*, published in 1776, a few months after the death of Hume.

Adam Smith's conversations with his friend David Hume about the political economy are likely to have influenced his book *The Wealth of Nations*.

See also //
31 Capitalism, p.66

Adam Smith // 1723–1790

3/Hack: Hume's thinking did much to establish the modern political economy, and anticipated the doctrines of his friend, Adam Smith.

No.13
The Spirit of the Laws

Montesquieu's influential vision

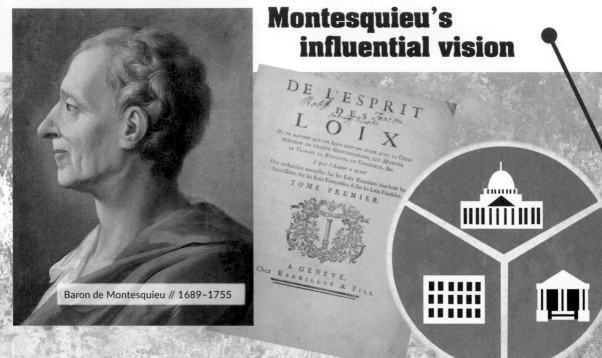

Baron de Montesquieu // 1689–1755

1/ Helicopter View: Born into a wealthy noble family in southwest France, Charles-Louis de Secondat, Baron de Montesquieu (1689–1755) spent his formative years in regional politics. In 1728, he embarked on 21 years of travelling around Europe researching and writing his most famous book, *The Spirit of the Laws*, first published in 1748. It contains a sweeping analysis of the relationship between the political systems he encountered during his journeys and their cultural, geographical and historical contexts. His insights led the founders of the United States of America – a country that did not exist at the time of his death – to formalize what was casually recognized in the English system and to construct a tripartite government on lines he recommended: a government divided into a President, a Congress and a Supreme Court. Having had such a profound influence on the instigators of this great nation, today the book stands as one of the most influential works of the Enlightenment.

Baron de Montesquieu's views were integral in providing the framework for government adopted by the United States of America.

2/ Shortcut: For Montesquieu, key components for successful government included a balanced constitutional system with a separation of powers, legal and civil liberties, and the end of slavery. His constitutional choices were republican (either democratic or aristocratic), monarchical or despotic. He believed that it was absolutely necessary for there to be a division of powers within the government, with separate legislative, executive and judicial branches, in order to provide checks and balances to maintain justice, limit corruption and encourage liberty within the nation and its laws. The final theory in *The Spirit of the Laws* is that geography and climate can influence the spirit of humans and societies. He believed that people living in warmer countries present a fiery, but vicious personality, whereas inhabitants of northern nations are braver, but cold and rigid. He further suggested that this spirit, in turn, inclines the population toward certain sorts of political and social institutions. Some regard this work as the first in the field of political sociology.

See also //
14 A Civil Society, p.32
16 The Federalist Papers, p.36
43 Presidential p.90
56 The Separation of Powers, p.116
83 The US Constitution, p.170

3/ Hack: *The Spirit of the Laws* stands as the founding work of modern comparative government.

No.14
A Civil Society
John Locke's liberal democracy

1/Helicopter View: One of the key issues of the Enlightenment in England was the battle for political power between Royalists and Parliamentarians that culminated in the English Civil War (1642–51). In his book of 1651, *Leviathan*, Thomas Hobbes had eloquently put the case in favour of the monarchy. The reply, equally well written, came from another British philosopher, the Parliamentarian John Locke (1632–1704), whose *Two Treatises of Government* were published in 1689. Though the two great thinkers agreed on the primacy of reason, the existence of a "state of nature" and the idea of a "social contract" to bind the people to authority, heavily influenced by their experiences of the horror of war, they took drastically different stances on the role of government and the rights of the people. The *First Treatise* directly opposed the divine rights of the monarch, but the second sought to justify the Glorious Revolution of 1688, which saw James II overthrown and William of Orange take the English throne on the condition that he was overseen by parliament.

John Locke's *Two Treatises of Government* was influential in justifying the replacement of James II by William and Mary.

William of Orange// 1650–1702

John Locke // 1632–1704

Queen Mary // 1662–94

2/ Shortcut: Locke's justification took the shape of the definition of a civil society. He places sovereignty in the hands of the people. For him, people are equal, have natural rights and live free from outside rule. Their behaviour is governed by natural law: they grow food, they gather in social groups, they trade, develop a common currency and form a community. Of course, Locke suggested, in these circumstances conflict was inevitable when one individual coveted another's property. So, in order for this civil society to work, people would need their property and liberties to be protected by laws and by a "legitimate" government that will enforce them. The government, which should comprise separate judicial, legislative and executive branches, would be beholden to the people. If it failed to work solely in the people's interest then they would have the right to dissolve it. Indeed, it would be their duty to rebel against it and replace it with one they trust. Locke's ideas were deeply influential on Thomas Jefferson (1743– 1826) as he drafted America's Declaration of Independence.

Thomas Jefferson agreed with Locke's assertion that government should benefit all of society.

See also //
11 Man's State of Nature, p.26
72 The Declaration of Independence, p.148

Thomas Jefferson // 1743–1826

IN CONGRESS, JULY 4, 1776.

The unanimous Declaration of the thirteen united States of America.

3/ Hack: Locke's theory of government based on the sovereignty of the people is central to the modern-day liberal-democratic state.

Power to the People
Jean-Jacques Rousseau's social contract

Jean-Jacques Rousseau // 1712–78

1/ Helicopter View: On its publication in 1762, *The Social Contract* was banned and copies were burned publicly in France and in the author's native Switzerland, his views on monarchy, governmental institutions and religion offending Catholics and Protestants alike. Thirty years later Jean-Jacques Rousseau (1712–78) was being celebrated in the streets of Paris by Maximilien Robespierre (1758–94) and his Jacobin revolutionaries, as they tore down the bloated trappings of the aristocracy. In the intervening years Rousseau's ideas had become well known through his popular writings, he had become a man of the people, a champion of the poor, and had led a life of constant struggle against oppression. His thinking was heavily influenced by both Thomas Hobbes's absolute monarchy and John Locke's liberalism, but differed significantly in its understanding of the concept of sovereignty. For Rousseau, the sovereign was not the ruler, it was the people. His purpose in writing *The Social Contract* was to explain his theory that in his era "Man is born free; and everywhere he is in chains" and to offer his ideas of how to break the chains and establish an effective political community for all.

Jean-Jacques Rousseau believed that people are inherently good but can be corrupted by their life experiences. His ideals of liberty, equality and fraternity were championed during the French Revolution.

2/ Shortcut: Rousseau's ideal society was based on a social contract freely entered into by all the individuals within it (defined as "the sovereign"), which would represent the "general will". Citizens would give up some of their rights in exchange for equality and freedom. However, the sovereign should have absolute authority only over matters of public interest. The role of the state was to ensure liberty and equality through its laws. Government (he suggests democracy, aristocracy or monarchy, depending on the size of the state), which was separate from the sovereign, would sort out day-to-day administration, which should always reflect the will of the sovereign. If the government were to exceed these boundaries, it would then be up to the people to abolish it. Rousseau's social contract looked to form a society that promoted "liberty, equality and fraternity", concepts still at the heart of politics in the modern world.

See also //
11 Man's State of Nature, p.26
14 A Civil Society, p.32
18 The *Ancien Régime*, p.34

Maximilien Robespierre // 1758–94

3/ Hack: Rousseau's social contract explains the importance of political participation and the danger of extreme inequalities.

No.16
The Federalist Papers
In defence of the US Constitution

Alexander Hamilton // 1757–1804

1/Helicopter View: In the years immediately following victory over the British in the American Revolutionary War (1775–83), the leading politicians and statesmen in the 13 states of the Union were engaged in serious debate about how to establish a good government in keeping with the Declaration of Independence that had been published on 4 July 1776. For some, the war had sowed the seeds of desire for a stronger union. For others, fears that a central authority could not adequately oversee such a large country saw them oppose such a move. The first written constitution, the Articles of Confederation, written in 1776–7 but not ratified until 1781, declared the states independent but under the authority of Congress. Despite attempts at amendment, the articles were perceived to be too weak. A new Constitution was drafted and submitted to the states for ratification in 1787, calling for three branches of national government: executive, legislative and judicial within a bicameral legislature with appropriate representation for the member states. It needed the approval of nine of the 13 states to be adopted.

Alexander Hamilton contributed 52 of the 85 Federalist Papers. The US Constitution was signed in Philadelphia on 17 September 1787.

2/Shortcut: The Federalist Papers were a series of 85 essays published in New York newspapers between 1787 and 1788 in support of urgent ratification. They were written by the celebrated statesmen Alexander Hamilton, James Madison and John Jay under the pseudonym "Publius". Debate raged over the constitutional principles involved in the new document. The articles detailed how the Constitution would work. They explained that the new system would preserve the Union, and, because of the checks and balances proposed, as a federal government Congress would act firmly and coherently in the national interest. Any conflicting interests, whether political or economic, between the states would be reconciled through representation in Congress, which, in turn, would be subject to judicial review and presidential veto. Whether the articles were influential on the public opinion of the day or not, on 21 June 1788 New Hampshire became the ninth state to ratify the Constitution and a year later, on 4 March 1789, government under the Constitution began.

See also //

43 Presidential, p.90

56 The Separation of Powers, p.116

72 The Declaration of Independence, p.148

83 The US Constitution, p.170

84 The Bill of Rights, p.172

3/Hack: The Federalist Papers are widely respected for their analysis of principles on which the government of the United States was established.

No.17
Origins of Conservative
Thought Edmund Burke's reflections

Edmund Burke // 1729–97

1/ Helicopter View: Edmund Burke (1729–97) was a statesman, orator and politician of some prominence during his lifetime, primarily because of his book, *Reflections on the Revolution in France*, published in 1790. Born and educated in Dublin, as a Whig member of Parliament (MP) in London he was recognized for championing the rights of parliament as opposed to those of the Crown, free markets, free trade and for his work on defining the role of an MP. Burke stressed the need for practicality in politics, and was thoroughly opposed to the traditional Enlightenment thinkers' theoretical speculation about humanity's "state of nature". For Burke, government should be a cooperative relationship between rulers and subjects based on the realities with which they were faced. He believed that, while the past was important, a willingness to adapt to the inevitability of change could, hopefully, reaffirm traditional values in changing circumstances.

2/Shortcut: In April 1775, open combat between British soldiers and the Massachusetts militia marked the beginning of the American Revolutionary War, the roots of which had been sown at least a decade before in growing philosophical and political differences. Surprisingly, Burke was vehement in his defence of the rebellious colonies, blaming British policies for provoking the crisis through their greed. For Burke, this was not a revolution; it was simply the act of a country justifiably defending its own interests. His response to the revolution in France was somewhat different, but sat neatly alongside his other liberal conservative opinions. In writing *Reflections*, his intention was to warn the people of England not to go down such a destructive path as the Jacobin revolutionaries. He wrote that in searching for equality, they had uprooted their political, social and cultural order, and replaced it with chaos via mob rule, spreading corruptions that were "usually the disease of wealth and power" to all ranks of life. He pointed out that no matter how angry the people were, they had to defer to the authority of tradition, relying instead on gradual change, order, private property and the moral order of the Christian religion.

Edmund Burke condemned the French Revolution as nothing but mob rule, while supporting justified resistance which, he claimed, had not amounted to a revolution In America.

See also //

3/Hack: Burke's mix of classical liberal and traditionalist views is now regarded as forming the roots of conservative thought.

No.18
The *Ancien Régime*
Out with the old, in with the new

Louis XVI // 1754-93

1/ Helicopter View:

The *Ancien Régime*, most often associated with early modern France, was a socio-political system common in many societies in the 17th and 18th centuries in which everyone was the subject of an absolute king. The rights of the people were determined by their social standing: at the top were the clergy, then came the nobility and finally the peasants. A common image of this society depicts rich, red-faced aristocrats enjoying fine food and wine in opulent dining rooms, while the poor, dressed in rags, fed up with searching the gutters for crusts of bread, finally had enough of it and called for revolution. Of course, there is some truth in this. The French Revolution, which began in 1789, led to the removal and eventual execution of the monarch – Louis XVI, changed the government, the administration, the military, the culture of the nation and brought an end to feudalism. There were also short-term causes, most particularly a financial crisis, partly caused by French involvement in the American Revolutionary War, which led to new, stringent tax laws. But, in reality, the end of the *ancien régimes* all over Europe was well underway before the revolutionary years.

The inability of Louis XVI to get France out of a financial crisis set in motion the revolution of 1789. He was guillotined for treason on 21 January 1793.

2/Shortcut: Historians have identified a number of long-term causes of the demise of the *Ancien Régime* in France. Rising literacy rates among the ordinary people led to an increase in learning, posing a threat to the monarchy, the state and the "old order". This also enabled a wider spread of the contemporary philosophies of the Enlightenment, either through the expansion of the book trade or via the first daily newspapers, which began publishing in Paris in 1777. This meant that more people were able to keep up to date with what was happening in government and even make their views felt if necessary through letters or pamphlets, particularly with the end of censorship. The establishment of a middle-class bourgeoisie, in effect an upper-class peasantry, many of whose members had made their money from mercantilism, also played a major role in disrupting the *Régime*'s natural order. Once they realized they had the power to ask for things they wanted, the system based on obedience fell apart. As the power of the monarchy declined, so did that of the Church. Into this power vacuum came the idea of a citizen, patriotic – not to the king – but to the state. The *Ancien Régime* was old news.

See also //

23 The Political Left, p.50

24 The Political Right, p.52

3/Hack: The *Ancien Régime* is a term used to describe the structure and politics of French society before the Revolution.

Pioneering the Women's Movement

Mary Wollstonecraft's dissent

Mary Wollstonecraft // 1759–97

1/ Helicopter View: The English intellectual, teacher and writer Mary Wollstonecraft (1759–97) is remembered today as Britain's first suffragist. Best known for her book, *A Vindication of the Rights of Woman* (1792), she was also a war reporter, spending time in Paris during the French Revolution, a prolific writer, a pedagogue, a radical republican, a single mother and a passionate lover. The thoughts she put forward in her book are now regarded as the first expression of feminist ideas. Her central argument was that men were in no way superior to women, and that if women were afforded the same opportunities and education, they would contribute as much to society as their male counterparts. But her writings were not concerned solely with women's issues, and encompassed education, the rights of all people and the encouragement of new thinking on the false distinctions of class, age and religion.

Wollstonecraft was born in Spitalfields, in London, but because of straitened circumstances, the family moved away. In 1774, she returned to London and founded a school for boys and girls near Newington Green, then the intellectual centre of Radical Dissenters. Mixing with these high-minded nonconformists challenged her thinking and helped shape her own emerging radical views.

Mary Wollstonecraft advocated giving girls and women access to the same educational opportunities as those available to men.

2/ Shortcut: In her most famous book, Wollstonecraft argues that true freedom demands equality of the sexes (to assert her credentials, in 1790 she had written *A Vindication of the Rights of Men*, written in direct response to Edmund Burke's *Reflections on the Revolution in France*). She suggests that intellect or reason is superior to emotion or passion and encourages women to acquire strength of mind and body rather than develop soft womanly virtues that are synonymous with weakness. She advocates education as the key for women to achieve the self-respect and self-image required to achieve their full capabilities. She was scathing about the work of Enlightenment thinkers like Jean-Jacques Rousseau because, while lauding the revolutionary idea that men should not have power over each other, they denied women that same basic right.

See also //
15 Power to the People, p.34
17 Origins of Conservative Thought, p.38
39 Feminism, p.82

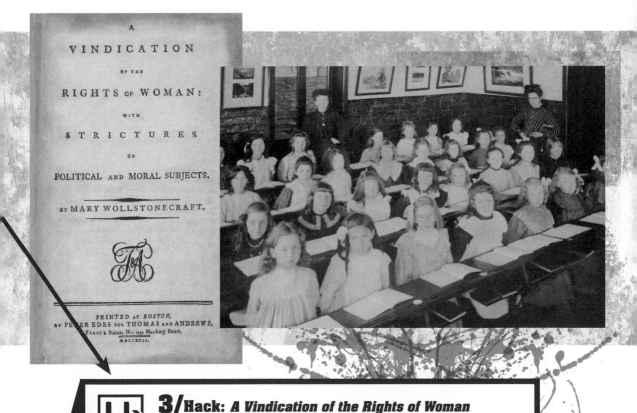

3/ Hack: *A Vindication of the Rights of Woman* is today regarded as one of the founding texts of liberal feminism.

No.20
The Pursuit of Happiness

Ethics of utilitarianism

Jeremy Bentham //
1748–1832

1/ Helicopter View: Although the notion that the morally right action produces the most good had been around since Classical Greece, the ethical system of utilitarianism – which determines morality on the basis of the greatest good for the greatest number – was first proposed and discussed by the English philosophers and economists Jeremy Bentham (1748–1832) and John Stuart Mill (1806–73). It was an attempt to answer a practical question: "What ought a man to do?" Bentham's answer, published in 1789, was that it is the consequences of human actions that count in evaluating their merit, and that their aims are twofold: the achievement of pleasure and the avoidance of pain. The happiness produced – its "utility" – is measurable by a calculus of felicity. The concept was developed further by Mill, who saw its political implications in terms of governments enabling citizens to pursue happiness. This is notably supported in a famous phrase from the US Constitution, which states that there are three inalienable rights given to all human beings by their Creator, and which governments should protect: "Life, Liberty and the pursuit of Happiness".

The effects of the Industrial Revolution provoked calls for social reform. One of the most popular theories was utilitarianism, associated with Jeremy Bentham and John Stuart Mill.

2/Shortcut: John Stuart Mill had lived his whole life as a utilitarian, having been heavily influenced by his father. In 1861, he published his views on the subject in serial form in *Fraser's Magazine.* His thinking revolves around a single notion: "Actions are right in proportion as they tend to promote happiness, wrong as they tend to produce the reverse of happiness." He argues that utilitarian sentiments exist naturally within human nature and that therefore, if society were to embrace acts that minimize pain and maximize happiness, an easy and natural code of ethics would develop for the good of those who lived by it. Governments making decisions in this way would create laws and policies that would allow the greatest happiness for the greatest number and the least unhappiness, whether by harm or by the restriction of liberty.

See also //
83 The US Constitution, p.170

John Stuart Mill // 1806–73

3/Hack: The central insight of utilitarianism is that one ought to promote happiness and prevent unhappiness whenever possible.

No.21
The Russian Revolution
Red star rises

1/ Helicopter View: At the beginning of the 20th century Russia was one of the poorest countries in Europe with a huge landless peasant class made up of many different ethnic groups, including Russians, Ukrainians, Poles, Germans, Jews and Finns. They were ruled over by an authoritarian czar, Nicholas II, and suffered under a repressive regime that was ruthlessly enforced. Industrialization came late in Russia, and unlike the majority of workers in the rest of Europe, those in Russia continued to be exploited as serfs to the land-owning nobility. When it eventually came, industrialization brought a new set of problems: a population boom, appalling conditions for the new class of workers and food shortages. It was no surprise that unrest, which had been simmering for years, finally broke the surface. An outcry following a massacre of protesting workers in St Petersburg in 1905 prompted promises of reform, but Russia's involvement in the First World War, with its associated casualties, food and fuel shortages, proved the final straw. In February 1917, demonstrators clamouring for bread took to the streets of St Petersburg (by then renamed Petrograd), supported by huge numbers of striking workers. Within five days the czar had abdicated and a provisional government was installed. However, the unrest continued.

Lenin became leader of the Bolsheviks in 1905. In February 1917, protesters took to the streets of Petrograd (above). Soldiers protested alongside workers. (opposite left).
In July 1918, the czar and his family were executed by the Bolsheviks (opposite right).

2/Shortcut: Inspired by Karl Marx (1818–83), a young lawyer, Vladimir Ilich Ulyanov (1870–924), known as Lenin, had become the leader of the Bolshevik revolutionary movement following the 1905 uprising. When the czar was deposed, Lenin saw his chance to mobilize the masses who had been drawn together through their suffering. Criticizing the newly formed provisional government, which was composed of leaders of the bourgeois liberal parties, he called for a Soviet government, one that would be ruled by soldiers, peasants and workers. A bloodless coup d'état, supported by disillusioned soldiers and millions of the newly established working class and known as the October Revolution, followed. Within days, Lenin became dictator of the world's first Communist state, which in 1923 was established as the Soviet Union.

See also //
27 Communism, p.58
28 Dialectical Materialism, p.60
71 The Communist Manifesto, p.146

3/Hack: In October 1917, the Bolshevik Party in Russia organized a victorious popular insurrection and established the first socialist workers' state in history.

No.22
Age of Extremes
The world at war: 1914–45

1/Helicopter View: Modern historians often regard the 20th century's two world wars as one single historical process. This view shines a new light on the failure of the governments and politicians involved to create a lasting peace in 1918. The horrors of the First World War are well documented. It drew in more than 30 countries and led to 40 million deaths. However, this was dwarfed by the Second World War, in which over 60 countries participated and which caused the deaths of more than 55 million people. Although the overall conflicts were global, both were fought primarily in Europe with the main protagonists being Britain, France and Russia (for much of the time) on one side and Germany, Austria and Hungary on the other. The economic cost was staggering with the countries ensnared in reparations and debt that rendered them incapable of returning to political and economic stability after 1918. But even these hideous statistics could not prevent the seeds of the second war being sown in the peace treaty signed at the end of the first.

2/ Shortcut: The Treaty of Versailles was signed in June 1919. The Allies were angry, putting full blame for the war on Germany and Austria-Hungary via the so-called War Guilt clause, exacting financial reparations of $33 billion ($2.3 trillion today), which led to massive hyperinflation and crippled the German economy (at a certain point one US dollar was worth one trillion marks), made worse still by the onset of the Great Depression. Germany lost all its overseas colonies and was asked to forfeit land for the formation of Poland. The size of its army and navy was reduced, the Rhineland demilitarized and the air force abolished. The German people were humiliated and resented the newly imposed government of the Weimar Republic for accepting such requirements. Although the Allied leaders thought they had brought a lasting peace to Europe, the harsh terms they imposed had put in place the perfect conditions for the rise of Hitler and the National Socialists.

Historians are convinced that the stringent terms set by the Treaty of Versailles at the end of the First World War (opposite) fuelled the animosity that led to the Second World War (below).

See also //

73 The Treaty of Versailles, p.150

3/ Hack: The political policies of the Allies at the end of the First World War were to blame for the advent of the Second World War.

No.23
The Political Left
A sharing society

1/ Helicopter View: The split between left and right in politics has its origins in the seating arrangements of members of the National Assembly during the French Revolution. As they met in Versailles in the summer of 1789, the delegates were deeply divided over the issue of how much power Louis XVI should have. During the debate, members of the aristocracy and other supporters of the monarchy sat on the right of the presiding officer, while on the left were the anti-royalist revolutionaries. Some historians suggest that this was a deliberate move to ease the counting of votes – there were over 500 delegates in the hall. Others argue it was simply pure chance that those in agreement sat together, to "avoid jeers from the galleries", and it could easily have been the other way around. The division was continued by the press, who began to refer to the "progressive" left and the "traditionalist" right, and by the mid-19th century the terms had become shorthand for two opposing political ideologies.

At the assembly in the Salle des États at the Hôtel des Menus-Plaisirs at Versailles, the aristocrats sat on the right of the king, while the commoners sat on the left.

2/Shortcut: Since then, the left, also known as liberal or progressive, has become closely associated with Socialism and, on the far left, Communism, as it believes that government should take care of all its citizens, particularly those who are seen as disadvantaged. It advocates state control of the major institutions of political and economic life. It tends to be hostile to the interests of traditional elites, like the wealthy and the aristocracy, and in favour of the working class. It also promotes the reform of social justice and the aim of creating a society with equal opportunities. Left-wing policies might also include taxation to redistribute opportunity and wealth, some kind of healthcare service, a welfare system, the introduction of laws against discrimination and assistance for those seeking employment.

The privations of the Great Depression saw the implementation of welfare systems in the United States, signed into law by President Roosevelt in 1935.

See also //

18 The *Ancien Régime,* p.40

24 The Political Right, p.52

25 Socialism, p.54

 3/Hack: Those on the left of the political spectrum tend to believe that wealth and power should be shared among all parts of society.

No.24
The Political Right
Authority, tradition and property

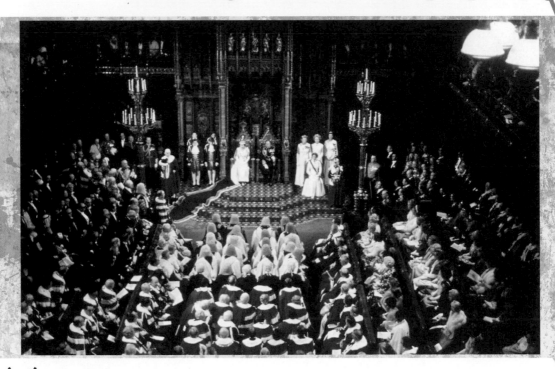

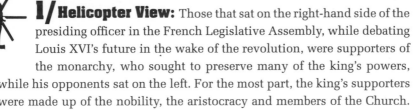**1/ Helicopter View:** Those that sat on the right-hand side of the presiding officer in the French Legislative Assembly, while debating Louis XVI's future in the wake of the revolution, were supporters of the monarchy, who sought to preserve many of the king's powers, while his opponents sat on the left. For the most part, the king's supporters were made up of the nobility, the aristocracy and members of the Church. Some historians point out that the choice of sides was deliberate as, according to Christian tradition, it is an honour to sit on the right-hand side of God, though others suggest it was down to chance. Whatever the truth, the practice continued, with those in favour of preserving the *Ancien Régime* on the right and the revolutionaries on the left, labels that are still in use in the political realm today.

The State Oening of the British parliament combines authority, tradition, pomp and ceremony.

2/Shortcut: Though the original right in France, *la droite*, was formed in defence of what had gone before, a system then under attack by the revolutionary Jacobins, it has retained a number of its original positions, particularly on authority, tradition and property. Those on the right believe the state should not interfere with individuals, promoting capitalism, which gives economic freedom to big business, with low taxes, a free market and as little regulation as possible. They tend toward the idea of the survival of the fittest, maintaining that social inequality is natural and normal. As a result, the idea of a class system where the richer employ the poorer is a healthy one, from which everyone benefits. Sometimes described as conservative – conserving what has gone before – and reactionary – as it tends to react to alternative, more radical movements – the right also encompasses nationalists, neo-conservatives and, at its extreme edge, Fascists.

For right wingers, a class system in which the rich employ the poor, such as in Rio de Janeiro, is one in which everyone benefits.

See also //

18 The *Ancien Régime*, p.40

23 The Political Left, p.50

30 Conservatism, p.64

3/Hack: Those on the right of the political spectrum tend to believe in tradition, as well as the preservation of personal wealth and private ownership.

No.25
Socialism Social ownership

1/ Helicopter View: Socialism is a populist economic and political system based on the public ownership of the means of production and distribution. It inhabits the left wing of the political spectrum. As an idea, it developed during the 1830s as a result of radical Enlightenment thinking and in opposition to the excesses and abuses of liberal individualism and capitalism that took place in the years after the Industrial Revolution. As some grew rich quickly, so others descended into poverty, causing financial inequality and other social concerns. A Socialist economy works through central planning rather than market forces, favouring production for use rather than purely for profit. Ideologically, Socialists assert moral authority over capitalism because it undermines democracy by facilitating exploitation and the unfair distribution of resources. Although heavily influenced by Karl Marx's thinking on Communism, Socialism rose to prominence because of Lenin's success in the Russian Revolution.

2/Shortcut: Historically in Europe, however, Socialism successfully pressed for universal suffrage, social reform, improved social conditions and a greater economic role for the state. In the 20th century, Socialism continued to remain a viable political system, although challenges, notably the increasing scarcity of natural resources and an expanding world population, weakened its traditional notions of economic growth and forced the movement's thinkers to confront its viability. New ideas included market Socialism, Christian Socialism and eco Socialism among others, but the most successful model was "democratic Socialism", which developed in Scandinavia during the years following the Second World War. The so-called Nordic Model, which borrows ideas freely from both sides of the political spectrum, refers to a set of policies that promote economic opportunities and security and a robust welfare state, within the framework of capitalism.

3/Hack: Socialism is an economic system based on the social ownership and operation of the means of production.

No.26
Democratic Socialism
The Nordic Model

 1/ Helicopter View: Perhaps the best example of democratic Socialism is the Nordic Model, so-called because it is used in Sweden, Norway, Finland, Iceland and Denmark. This political system, sometimes referred to as the "third way" because it mixes parts of Socialism with capitalism, was developed in Scandinavia during the years following the Second World War when struggling economies needed to increase their competitiveness in a new world market. Today these countries boast high living standards and low income disparity, a much-desired combination of economic opportunity and equality. The model marries free-market capitalism with a sophisticated social benefits system. Substantial taxation allows the state to provide free good-quality education and healthcare as well as guaranteed pensions, which are administered by the government for the benefit of all citizens. There is considerable gender equality, resulting in a great degree of engagement in the workplace for women and a significant level of parental involvement by men. Relaxed employment laws enable companies to release workers when necessary who, in turn, are supported by generous welfare programmes until they find work. Taxes are high but people are willing to pay them because of the benefits they generate.

Since the Second World War, the Nordic countries have put in place social programmes that make individuals feel secure.

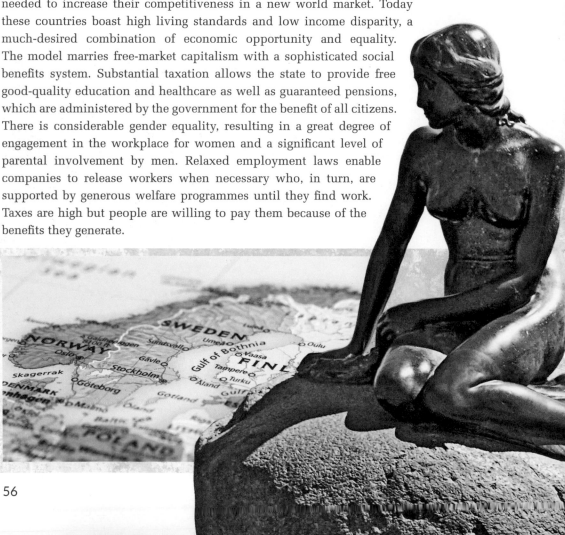

2/Shortcut: The system does have its critics. Some maintain that it is not Socialist at all; others highlight the relatively poor GDP and the high carbon footprint of economies with a dependence on natural resources. They also point to issues of sustainability in the face of an ageing population, to increased immigration and the poor global economic conditions, all of which are likely to put pressure on the state's tax income. Despite the criticism, this form of democratic Socialism has proved highly successful on a social level, with five Scandinavian countries appearing in the top ten of the UN's list of happiest countries in which to live in 2017.

See also //
23 The Political Left, p.50
25 Socialism, p.54

3/Hack: Democratic Socialism blends Socialist and democratic methods together to build a workable social, political and economic system.

Communism The classless society

Vladimir Lenin // 1870–1924

Mao Zedong // 1893–1976

Nikita Khrushchev // 1894–1971

1/Helicopter View: In traditional terms, Communism is the principle of the communal ownership of all property. For example, in a primitive community, basic economic resources (such as land, boats, tools, etc.) belonged to the community as a whole rather than individuals or families. Modern-day Communism, however, is specifically linked to the ideas of two German economists, Karl Marx (1818-83) and Friedrich Engels (1820–95) who published *The Communist Manifesto* in 1848. In it they blamed society's problems on the unequal distribution of wealth between the bourgeoisie and the proletariat. Their solution to the problem, and to bring about happiness and prosperity to everyone, was to eliminate the distinction between rich and poor through the abolition of private property. Since the rich would never give up their goods or status voluntarily, it was up to the poor – or working class – to rise up and take it anyway. A dictatorship of the proletariat would follow, during which time the state would wither away, any differences between manual and intellectual labour, between rural and urban life, would disappear and be replaced by a classless society. For Marx and Engels this process was inevitable because of capitalism's inherent instability. The new Communist society would be regulated by the principle "from each according to his ability, to each according to his needs."

Prime movers in the world of Communism have included Lenin and Khrushchev (Soviet Union), Mao (China), Che Guevara and Castro (Cuba) and Ho Chi Minh (Vietnam).

2/ Shortcut: During the 20th and 21st centuries, Communism has been successful in many countries. Following the revolution, Russia remained a Communist state for more than 70 years, but it was not the state envisaged by Marx or Lenin. Promises made by the government to the people that it would supply them with all they needed to live comfortably were not met. Corruption flourished as the socio-economic situation grew worse and in 1991 Communism was voted out of the political regime. Of course, there still are Communist governments in many parts of the world, including China, Cuba, Laos, North Korea and Vietnam. Although the old Communist notions have been discredited, the sense of injustice that animated them in the first place is still very much alive.

See also //
21 The Russian Revolution, p.46
28 Dialectical Materialism, p.60
49 Dictatorship, p.102
71 The Communist Manifesto, p.146

Che Guevara // 1928–1967

Fidel Castro // 1926–2016

Ho Chi Minh // 1890–1969

 3/ Hack: Communism is a political philosophy that aims to create a classless, stateless, egalitarian society in which all decision-making is done democratically.

No.28
Dialectical Materialism
Conflict and change

Karl Marx // 1818–83

Freidrich Engels // 1820–95

1/ Helicopter View: Dialectical materialism is the official philosophy of Communism. Based on the writings of Karl Marx and Friedrich Engels, it is a way of understanding reality, whether through thoughts, emotions or the material world. In essence, this methodology – a mixture of dialectics and materialism – proposes that all thinking, all institutions, all culture, all politics are basically reflecting and acting on the everyday conditions of life that we experience. These "material" conditions change over time as a consequence of human beings thinking about them. This process of the conditions we are born with or into and how we perceive and change them is the materialist interpretation of history. Dialectics, of which Marx took much from the writings of German philosopher Georg Hegel (1770–1831), is the simple idea that everything changes. Every notion contains some inherent contradiction or conflict: a thesis gives rise to an antithesis, which leads to the development of a new, more sophisticated notion.

2/Shortcut: Dialectical materialism looks at history in the following way: our conditions determine our thinking. The main thing about our conditions in the last 12,000 years is the fact that some people have access to resources and others do not. This causes a conflict in society. Everyone constantly thinks about their conditions, but different classes come to different conclusions. The ones who have access to resources do not want change; those who do not have access to resources do. Change comes about when the latter win against the former (revolution). The whole cycle then starts again with new classes and new conditions. After the Russian Revolution in 1917, the proper interpretation of dialectical materialism became a subject of state policy. The Soviet version of dialectical materialism, as codified by Joseph Stalin (1878–1953), was known as *diamat*. It became the official philosophy of the Soviet state and had a major influence on Soviet intellectual tradition.

Based on the writings of Karl Marx and Friedrich Engels, dialectical materialism is the theoretical foundation of Communism.

See also //

21 The Russian Revolution, p.46

27 Communism, p.58

71 The Communist Manifesto, p.146

3/Hack: Dialectical materialism holds that everything is constantly changing and evolving.

No.29
Liberalism/Centrism
The big tent

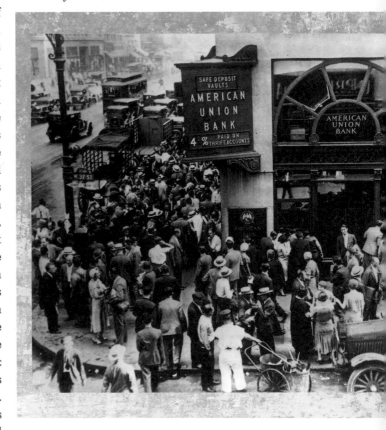

1/ Helicopter View: Like Socialism, liberalism is difficult to define, as people who call themselves "liberals" hold a wide array of differing views, depending on their principles. This has led to a common description of it as the "big tent". However, for the purposes of this book, liberalism – or centrism – is the political philosophy that occupies the middle ground of the political spectrum. Originating in the 18th century, the movement is historically associated with the idea that freedom – of the individual, of political institutions, of religion, of enterprise and of economics – would best fit a society based on democracy and liberty. It reached its peak as a political force in the early years of the 20th century, before the horrors of the First World War and the Great Depression that followed brought a temporary halt to ideas of a more humane world. As a political philosophy, however, liberalism remains popular, most notably because of its insistence on conscience and justice in politics. Liberals support ideas and programmes such as freedom of speech, freedom of the press, freedom of religion, free markets, civil rights, democratic societies, secular governments and international cooperation. The liberal movement promotes toleration, the rights of racial and religious minorities and the rights of individuals to be consulted in decisions that directly affect them.

2/Shortcut: The end of the Cold War ushered in a period of political liberalism in many parts of the world, which saw the economies of China and India develop rapidly, the Soviet Union implode, the Nordic countries adopt free markets and state powers begin to shrink to the benefit of corporations and NGOs. But the 9/11 terror attacks in 2001 put an end to the trend. Since then the War on Terror has seen civil liberties under increasing pressure, democracy in Russia in decline again, freedom of speech in China curtailed and an economic crisis in Europe and the USA, all of which have allowed the power of the state to rise once more. In recent years, liberalism has been regarded by some as fence sitting, avoiding political extremes and promoting moderate policies in order to maximize electoral support, particularly among swing voters with no traditional allegiances. Today, for others, liberalism remains a bulwark against the rise of right-wing populism.

The First World War and the Great Depression shook people's faith in liberal values, as did the 9/11 terror attacks. In the UK, Saffiyah Khan (below left) became a symbol of resistance against racism in 2017.

See also //

40 Terrorism, p.84

3/Hack: Liberalism is a broad political ideology based on the values of individual liberty, equality and economic freedom.

No.30
Conservatism Respecting authority

Robert Peel // 1788–1850

Benjamin Disraeli // 1804–81

Winston Churchill // 1874–1965

Theodore Roosevelt // 1858–1919

1/Helicopter View: One of the major political movements in the last 200 years, Conservatism expresses a preference for the old and established social and political order. Its advocates stress the importance of respect for authority, tradition, prescription and continuity, looking to history to find the way forward rather than to the abstract or the ideal. This idea rests on the premise that society is a living organism that has evolved organically and therefore has developed institutions and practices that suit it. It does not reject change completely, but insists that changes should be organic rather than revolutionary. For Conservatives, the government's role is to be the servant and not the master of the existing ways of life and that it should accept what is rather than try and transform it into something else. Conservatives support capitalism, through the preservation of private wealth and private ownership, and emphasize the importance of the self-reliance of the individual. They tend to hold traditional religious views, recommend strong punishments for law-breakers and have little time for minority groups.

The many faces of Conservatism, from Robert Peel to Donald Trump.

2/ Shortcut: Historians usually point to the reaction to events during the French Revolution in 1789 as the starting point for Conservatism. Edmund Burke, now regarded as the father of the movement, argued forcefully against the uprising in his book *Reflections on the Revolution in France* (1790), in which he stressed the importance of inherited institutions and customs such as the monarch, the family and the Church. Today, Conservatism in Europe is often represented by the Christian Democrats, who advocate market-led economics, membership of the European Union and strong defence policies, ideas supported by the British Conservative Party until the 2017 in/out referendum on Europe. In the USA, the movement is generally represented by the Republican Party, most recently during the presidencies of Ronald Reagan (1981–89) and George W. Bush (2001–09). It is particularly strong in the nation's rural heartland and less so in the more liberal cities and college towns.

See also //

17 Origins of Conservative Thought, p.38

24 The Political Right, p.52

31 Capitalism, p.66

Margaret Thatcher // 1925–2013

Ronald Reagan // 1911–2004

Angela Merkel // b. 1954

Donald Trump // b. 1946

3/ Hack: Conservatism is a political doctrine that believes in the value of traditional institutions and practices.

No.31
Capitalism
Driving economic growth

1/Helicopter View: Capitalism has been the dominant economic system in the Western world since the end of feudalism in the 16th century. In essence, it is a system in which the factors of production (the setting up and running of a business; capital goods, including property; natural resources) are owned by private companies (or individuals). The companies derive their income from this ownership, which allows them to operate as they wish, keeping their processes efficient and maximizing profits. They benefit from a free market economy, which operates according to the law of supply and demand. Companies compete with each other in the market to make the greatest profit, selling their goods for the highest price while keeping costs as low as possible. When demand for a particular good grows, prices rise, prompting businesses to increase production. This, in turn, adds to the supply, which causes prices to fall again. The dance continues until only the most successful companies remain. Another important aspect of capitalism is the financial markets, where businesses attract investors and raise capital to expand.

Wall Street represents American economic might, as powerful an icon for capitalism as the Statue of Liberty is for freedom.

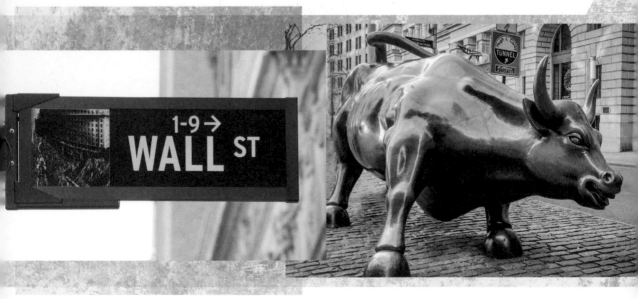

2/ Shortcut: Since the theory of "capitalism" was first discussed by Adam Smith (1723–90) in *The Wealth of Nations* (1776) (the term itself was not in use until 1854, in a novel by William Makepeace Thackeray), it has proved a very effective system of driving economic growth. So much so that although government is a public, not private, institution its role is now to use taxes and other resources to provide a legal framework, some regulation and the necessary security in which companies can conduct their business freely. Capitalism has been successful for a number of reasons: economic freedom helps political freedom; it incentivizes companies to produce what consumers want at prices that produce profit; and it encourages competition, innovation, economic growth and a higher standard of living. However, there are disadvantages too. Such a system can create a gap between the ultra-wealthy and the workers, it can lead to unfair pay and unsafe working conditions as companies chase profits, and capitalistic companies are less concerned with environmental issues.

See also //

77 Tax and Spend, p.150

81 The 99 percent Movement, p.166

88 Trades/Labour Unions, p.180

97 Climate Change, p.198

3/ Hack: Capitalism is an economic and political system in which a country's trade and industry are controlled by private owners for profit.

Patriotism
Love and respect your country

 **1/ Helicopter View:** One thing many political terms have in common is that they have different meanings for different people. Patriotism is no exception. A vox pop on any street asking what it meant would elicit a variety of answers. In fact, its meaning – love of one's country – harks back to ancient Greece and Rome, when citizens were duty-bound to show loyalty to the *patris* or *patria* (homeland), as part of the search for the common good. Today the word implies a much more emotional and sentimental attachment to one's country of birth. It is perceived as an inherently defensive notion. It has nothing to do with a country's ruling powers and all to do with loving a particular place, its culture, its history and its particular way of life. Critics point to the similarities between patriotism and nationalism, something that George Orwell (1903–50) addressed in his essay "Notes on Nationalism", published in 1945. He outlined a specific difference between the two ideologies: "Patriotism is of its nature defensive, both militarily and culturally. Nationalism, on the other hand, is inseparable from the desire for power."

All countries have their own national symbols, which are used to unite people in times of celebration and also in times of war.

2/Shortcut: In reality, patriotism has to be about more than blind loyalty to one's country. It cannot be that everyone believes their own country to be the best, because only one country could qualify for such a title. Perhaps, then, it is more about pride in one's country of origin and a desire to play your part in helping that country to thrive, for which one has to act in the country's best interests and not simply your own. A country could be compared to a family: without love and respect, the family could break apart, as could a country riven by argument, disagreement and social unrest. Your duty therefore as a citizen, no matter where you are from, is to be patriotic by focusing on what is good, and by pushing for progress with love and respect.

See also //

33 Nationalism, p.70

3/Hack: Patriotism is the passive expression of love for one's own country.

No.33
Nationalism Desire for power

1/Helicopter View: Nationalism is a modern movement that sits on the far right of the political spectrum. It emerged at the end of the 18th century following the French Revolution and the American Revolutionary War. Before that communities had formed around a town, city, kingdom or religion. Nationalism is based on the idea that each community should establish its own "nation" state, which would be made up of all members of that nationality who are likely to share ethnicity, culture, religion or social values. The corresponding ideology of such nations, particularly in the latter part of the 19th century, believed that theirs was superior to all others. This superiority assumed aggressive and intolerant forms and minorities from other ethnic or religious groups within the nation were often persecuted. Furthermore, this superiority could extend to arrogance and aggression, with some nationalists believing they have a right to extend power over another nation. In the 20th century nationalism became an essential element in popularizing Fascism and other totalitarian movements, as well as occasionally acting as a positive force for national cohesion against oppression, such as in India and Vietnam, and establishing the independence of a minority group within a larger nation, such as the Basques and the Catalans in Spain.

In a 1945 essay, George Orwell (centre) condemned nationalism, as exemplified by Nazi Germany (below). However, in Egypt in the 1950s, a nationalist movement led to a positive outcome with the overthrow of a corrupt monarchy (below left).

2/ Shortcut: Today, during a time of political upheaval and economic uncertainty, nationalism is alive and well, particularly in Europe and America where voters are facing a number of challenges: austerity, unemployment, job insecurity, fear of immigration and a general sense of vanishing influence over the decisions that affect their daily lives. The result for many has been a search for who to blame for this and the right-wing political parties have been quick to take advantage of what is seen as a new form of populist nationalism, which pins the responsibility for all these ills on the free movement of workers and high levels of immigration.

A Catalan independence rally at the Nou Camp stadium in Barcelona, 2013.

See also //
32 Patriotism, p.68

3/ Hack: Nationalism is an ideology in which people believe their nation is superior to all others.

No.34
Imperialism What's yours is mine

1/Helicopter View: Imperialism – the process of domination of a weak nation by a strong one, usually by force and for material gain – is the ideology behind colonialism. But, in the modern world, these two words and the concepts behind them have gone out of fashion, even though echoes of their existence remain, not the least of which are in the foreign policies of the world's superpowers. The fact is that imperialism has been the most powerful ideology in world history for the last 500 years. Of course, the process has a longer history than that. The Persians, the Macedonians, the Romans and the Mongols all left their own shores to plunder elsewhere in search of gold and glory. The idea caught on. Bigger ships and better weaponry, particularly among the European nations, saw Britain, France, Spain, Portugal and the Netherlands build empires in the Americas, India and the East Indies. With such power came influence, money, natural resources and cheap labour.

In the 18th century, the Industrial Revolution increased demand for raw materials and new markets in which to sell products, giving imperialism further impetus into Africa and Asia. At its height, the British Empire, on which it was said "the sun never set", covered over 36 million square kilometres (14 million square miles) of territory in which over 450 million people – more than a quarter of the world's population – lived. It encompassed India, Canada, Australia, some parts of Africa and the South Pacific.

Cecil Rhodes (1853–1902), a great believer in British imperialism, depicted bestriding the African continent.

72

2/Shortcut: Although there are those who look back to the Age of Imperialism with some pride, pointing out positive legacies such as governance, laws, stability, transport networks and educational systems, public opinion turned firmly against the idea during the 20th century for a number of reasons. The carnage of war in the trenches and the brutality of Nazi atrocities, all carried via mass communication that graphically portrayed the horrors of war and oppression, prompted widespread moral revulsion. By 1945, the act of fighting for democracy and freedom no longer sat well with the notion of empire, the economic advantages of which by then had run their course.

Britain, Germany, Russia, France and Japan contemplated their slice of China in the 1890s, while Columbia put on a US warship hat, called *World Power*, in 1901.

See also //

35 Militarism/ Pacifiscm, p.74

3/Hack: Imperialism is the exercise of power by a state beyond its borders.

No.35
Militarism/Pacifism
War and peace

1/Helicopter View: The *New Oxford American Dictionary* defines militarism as "the belief or desire of a government or people that a country should maintain a strong military capability and be prepared to use it aggressively to defend or promote national interests". Prime examples of countries that pursue this policy in the modern world are the USA, North Korea, Russia and Israel. The US spends some 50 percent of its federal budget on defence. The much-vaunted F-35 fighter-bomber, which became operational at the beginning of 2018, will cost an estimated $1 trillion to buy, operate and support during its lifetime. North Korea was founded in 1953, as a result of the Korean War; its birth from conflict is now used as justification for the prioritizing of military spending. Nearly 25 percent of its government budget goes on the military and some 40 percent of its population is on active or reserve military duty. Combined, they form the largest military force in the world, with over six million members. In contrast, pacifism is opposition to war, militarism and violence, and holds the belief that disputes should be resolved peacefully. There have been advocates of pacifism throughout history, often based on grounds of religion, morality or the practical belief that war is wasteful and ineffective. A major proponent of the idea of non-violence, Mahatma Gandhi (1869–1948), was a central figure in the Indian independence movement. His campaign of protest and fasting helped achieve freedom in 1947. His work inspired others, among them Martin Luther King Jr. (1929–68), who led the civil rights movement against racial segregation in the USA, and the founders of the Campaign for Nuclear Disarmament.

North Korea boasts the world's biggest military force. Gandhi called non-violence "a weapon for the brave".

2/ Shortcut: Supporters of militarism believe it is the best system for protecting a nation's interests. It also provides employment and education to some and wealth to a few. Opponents point to the high costs, the suffering, the environmental destruction and the poor results. Pacifists are of the view that it is wrong to kill unless you have no choice and maintain that there are no true victors in war. Critics ask what a pacifist would do when faced with someone ready to kill them, highlighting the immorality of sitting back and doing nothing in the face of invasion and that sometimes war can bring resolution.

See also //
8 The Just War Theory, p.20
34 Imperialism, p.72
76 "I Have A Dream", p.156

 3/ Hack: Militarism places great importance on military power; pacifism sees no justification for war.

Fascism
Out of the ashes

1/Helicopter View: Fascism, considered to be at the far-right end of the political spectrum, is characterized by authoritarianism, nationalism and xenophobia. It is often a one-party dictatorship, with government control of industry and commerce and the forcible suppression of opposition by the military or a secret police force. It states that the national interest supersedes all others, sacrificing the welfare of individuals to achieve its social goals. It also seeks to restore the nation to "purity" by "internal cleansing and external expansion". Fascism was born in the early years of the 20th century, flourished during a period of European political turmoil, and then all but disappeared when the Red Flag was raised over the Reichstag in Berlin on 8 May 1945, signalling Adolf Hitler's defeat.

Mussolini and Hitler, pictured together in Berlin in 1937, General Franco of Spain (above) and Sir Oswald Mosely (opposite), shown with members of the British Union of Fascists in 1936.

2/ Shortcut: The idea of Fascism has its roots in 19th century anti-liberalism, but the first Fascist government won power in Italy in 1922, led by Benito Mussolini (1883–1945). He was elected prime minister of a country devastated by war, with high inflation and unemployment rates. Despite being on the winning side in 1918, Italy had not benefited from the Treaty of Versailles and Mussolini was able to foster this injustice, together with the fear of Communism that followed Bolshevik success in Russia, to articulate a new nationalism for Italians, particularly among war veterans, offering the vision of a strong country with a future. In January 1925, Italy was declared a Fascist state with Mussolini as Il Duce. His regime, held together by strong state control enforced by his brutal Blackshirts, and by his cult of personality, attempted to re-establish Italy as a great European power. Military actions in Libya, Somalia, Ethiopia and Albania had echoes of the Roman Empire, but left Mussolini's armed forces exhausted. Mussolini provided military support to Franco in the Spanish Civil War before signing a Pact of Steel with Hitler in 1939. Italy joined the war against the Allies in 1940 but its military weakness was exposed. In 1945, shortly before Hitler's defeat, Mussolini was captured and shot by Italian insurgents. However, his ideas and practices influenced other Fascist movements, in Germany, Spain, France and elsewhere.

The Fascist symbol, a bundle of rods and an axe blade known as the fasces, is an ancient Roman symbol representing the power of life and death.

See also //

33 Nationalism, p.70

37 National Socialism, p.78

3/ Hack: Fascism is a conservative form of government that prioritizes the state above all else.

No.37
National Socialism
A new world order

1/Helicopter View: National Socialism, better known as Nazism, is taken from the name "Nationalsozialistische Deutsche Arbeiterpartei" (National Socialist Workers' Party), a political party so-named by Adolf Hitler (1889–1945) when he became its leader in 1921. A party with far-right tendencies and many policies in common with Mussolini's Fascist Party, it added the word "Socialist" to its name to draw workers away from Communism and toward populist nationalism. Promoting national pride, dissatisfaction with the terms of the Treaty of Versailles – which were crippling the economy – and anti-Semitism, the party prospered. In 1929, following the stock market crash in New York, Europe suffered further economic depression and unemployment. Hitler championed his party's aims in a series of fiery speeches blaming Communists and Jews for everything, swelling the ranks of the party, particularly with young, economically disadvantaged Germans. In 1932, the Nazi Party won 230 of 608 seats in the Reichstag and Hitler became chancellor the following year. He immediately started undoing the terms of the Treaty of Versailles in an effort to restore Germany's standing in the world. He strengthened the armed forces, annexing Austria and invading Czechoslovakia in order to provide *Lebensraum* (living space) for the country's expanding population. In 1939, Germany invaded Poland, and Great Britain and France declared war.

The Nazis recruited boys over the age of ten for the Hitler Youth movement (above). From 1942 until the end of the war, hundreds of thousands of Jews were sent to their deaths in concentration camps (opposite).

78

2/ Shortcut: Nazi rule was brutal from the outset. All other political parties were banned, and in 1933 they opened Dachau, the first concentration camp, to house political prisoners. In time, this included Jews, artists and intellectuals, gypsies, the physically and mentally handicapped and homosexuals, all groups that did not fit in with Hitler's ideas of the racial purity of the new Germany. It was particularly in views on racial superiority that Nazism differed from Fascism. As war approached, the anti-Jewish campaigns increased. During the invasions of both Poland and Russia, tens of thousands of Jews were slaughtered or sent to the death camps. In 1942, as part of the "Final Solution", the Nazis began deporting thousands of Jews from all parts of occupied Europe to camps such as Auschwitz and Dachau where they were gassed. When the war finally ended in April 1945, some six million Jews had died.

See also //

8 The Just War Theory, p.20

22 Age of Extremes, p.48

36 Fascism, p.76

49 Dictatorship, p. 102

73 The Treaty of Versailles. p.150

 3/ Hack: National Socialism was the political ideology of the German Nazi Party.

No.38
Anarchy
The absence of government

1/ Helicopter View: Today, anarchy is often understood to mean chaos and disorder due to the absence of authority and is feared for its bomb-throwing lawlessness. In fact, the word "anarchy" – taken from the ancient Greek *an*, meaning "without", and *archos*, meaning "leader" – suggests a society based around the absence of a leader or ruling class, proposing instead a self-managed society with an emphasis on equality and the freedom of the individual. Anarchy harks back to the era of the hunter-gatherer for whom society was a small band of humans, without hierarchy or authority. The last remaining anarchist societies are said to be the San (Bushmen) and the Pygmies from south and central Africa and the Australian Aborigines. As a political force, the idea of anarchism grew out of the rubble of the French Revolution, for which the monarch and the government were held responsible. People were looking for alternatives to what they saw as theocracy, perhaps a system that would eliminate authoritarianism and instead allow equality. Anarchy, basically a workers' movement, offered freedom, egalitarianism and peace. Today's anarchists propose a society of small, local communities based on decentralization, individualism and mutual aid. The American linguist, Noam Chomsky (b. 1928), who describes himself as an anarcho-syndicalist, describes it as "a conception of a very organized society...with as little control and domination as is feasible".

On the day of President Trump's inauguration in 2017 members of the radical anti-Fascist movement were labelled as violent anarchists, while others called the new president an anarchist for ignoring the rules of government.

2/Shortcut: Because there are many forms of state control, today there are many different forms of anarchy, such as anarcha-feminism, green anarchism and anarcho-pacifism. These movements have little in common except for holding the state responsible for patriarchy and oppression, environmental damage and unnecessary political violence respectively. Although they all agree that the state should be done away with, they cannot agree how to achieve it. Many people believe that anarchy is a good idea, in theory; Mahatma Gandhi (1869–1948) once said, "The ideal non-violent state will be an ordered anarchy", but perhaps Chomsky's observation that it is an "unrealistic utopian theory" rather than a stand-alone system of government explains its failure to succeed.

See also //

18 The *Ancien Régime*, p.40
50 Theocracy, p.104

3/Hack: Anarchy is a state of being without any government or authority.

Feminism
The longest revolution

1/Helicopter View: Although there had been rumblings of discontent throughout history, women's participation in the French Revolution was the catalyst for modern-day feminism. The movement was spurred by the writings of Mary Wollstonecraft (1759–97), whose *A Vindication of the Rights of Woman* (1792) argued that women should have the same rights as men, including education, earnings and property. Today, historians divide the women's movement into three waves. The first peaked early in the 20th century with women earning the right to vote, the right to own property apart from a husband, rights to education and employment, and fairer marriage laws. In the 1940s, the war boosted the involvement of women in the workplace. The publication in 1949 of the best-selling book *The Second Sex* by Simone de Beauvoir (1908–86) questioned how women were viewed in society in the light of the war years and led indirectly to the second wave, which began in the 1960s. This included the passing of the Equal Pay and the Civil Rights Acts, and the introduction of the contraceptive pill, which enabled women to delay or prevent childbirth and establish careers if they chose. The third wave began in the 1990s, aiming at the inclusion of all women, reducing the gender pay gap, ending violence against women and getting rid of the "glass ceiling".

Emmeline Pankurst (above left) was a leader of the women's suffrage movement for 40 years. British women finally won equal voting rights in 1928.

2/Shortcut: The fight for equality is far from over. In 2017, the #MeToo social media movement hit the headlines, highlighting the prevalence of sexual harassment and violence in the workplace. The movement was founded in 2006 by civil rights activist Tarana Burke but was revitalized when the American actress Alyssa Milano tweeted: "If all the women who have been sexually harassed or assaulted wrote 'Me too' as a status, we might give people a sense of the magnitude of the problem," and received 30,000 replies overnight. Shortly afterwards a news story broke, concerning allegations of sexual abuse of the film producer Harvey Weinstein, which has triggered similar accusations against powerful men around the world as thousands of women were empowered to share their experiences of harassment and worse. In early 2018, the Time's Up movement was set up in response to the scandal. Only time will tell whether these recent movements represent the fourth wave of feminism.

During the second wave of the women's movement, in the 1960s and 1970s, feminists fought for women's rights and in defence of the abortion law. During this time, Gloria Steinem (below) became a spokeswoman for the American women's movement.

See also //

19 Pioneering the Women's Movement, p.42

3/Hack: Feminism is a belief in the social, political and economic equality of the sexes.

No.40
Terrorism The end of innocence

1/Helicopter View: At 8.45am on Tuesday 11 September 2001, an American Airlines Boeing 767 crashed into the north tower of the World Trade Center in New York City. Within moments satellites were beaming images of the scene around the world, so millions were watching as, 18 minutes later, a second plane flew into the south tower and exploded. What had initially seemed like a horrific accident had suddenly become something infinitely more sinister. At 9.45, a third plane ploughed into the Pentagon in Virginia and shortly after that a fourth crashed in a field in Pennsylvania, short of its intended target of Washington, DC. By 10.30 that morning, the Twin Towers had collapsed in a massive cloud of dust and smoke. In all 2,996 people were killed in what became known as the 9/11 attacks, including all the airline passengers and crews and the 19 terrorists involved, and more than 6,000 were injured. Only six people in the Twin Towers at the time of their collapse survived. In the coming days, the extremist Islamic group Al-Qaeda claimed responsibility, stating that the attacks were in revenge for US support of Israel, the presence of US troops in Saudi Arabia and sanctions against

Iraq. The economic cost of the attacks was estimated at $3 trillion. In 2004, Osama bin Laden (1957–2011) admitted his leadership of the operation. It was the most effective act of terrorism in recorded history.

2/ Shortcut: Terrorism is defined as the unlawful use of violence and intimidation, especially against civilians, in the pursuit of political aims. The 9/11 attacks were tactically successful, spreading fear by killing hundreds of innocent people and grabbing headlines all over the world, but bin Laden's aim had been to encourage American withdrawal from the Middle East and this did not happen. Instead, the US launched the War on Terror. Around the world countries strengthened anti-terrorism laws and expanded intelligence agencies that have successfully countered further terrorist attacks. Although terrorism still creates headlines and fear, it continues to be unable to achieve any of its stated goals.

Mohamad Atta (below right) was one of the ringleaders of the 19 terrorists that carried out the 9/11 attacks on the World Trade Center.

See also //
29 Liberalism/ Centrism, p.62
90 Radicalism, p.184

 3/ Hack: Terrorism is the use of violence to create fear for political, religious or ideological reasons.

No.41
Democracy The will of the people

1/ Helicopter View: Democracy was the single most successful political idea in the 20th century. As a concept, it is simple and fair: a system that encourages citizens to express their political preferences through free and fair elections, has constraints on the power of the executive, lives by the rule of law that applies equally to all its citizens, and gives a guarantee of civil liberties; in other words, government of the people, by the people, for the people. It has been around a long time, the first example being the popular assembly of ancient Athens, which began sometime in the 4th century BCE. The last 200 years have seen a steady rise in the number of the world's democracies as a result of the end of empires, the horrors of two world wars and the break-up of the Soviet Union in 1991. In 2015, it was estimated that as many as four billion people live in democratic societies, in Europe, the Americas, Africa, Asia, Australia, New Zealand, Japan and Mongolia.

Elections are an essential part of democracy but no guarantee of its efficacy. Despite almost 250 years of democracy some critics say that America is actually a plutocracy – a state ruled by wealth.

2/ Shortcut: With so many democratic systems now in existence, the spectrum is so broad that few countries actually deserve to be called true democracies. Even countries like the United States, which has always regarded itself as a beacon of democracy, is criticized for not giving all people equal power in the government. Linguist and political observer Noam Chomsky (b. 1928) claims that the lower 70 percent have no influence on policy and that the economic elite call the shots. He says that, in fact, America is not a democracy at all; it is a plutocracy – a state ruled by wealth. Although many countries do have democratic aspects to their government, most commentators agree that the Nordic countries – Norway, Sweden and Iceland – score best in terms of government accountability to the people. UK Prime Minister Winston Churchill (1874–1965) once said, "Democracy is the worst form of government, except for all the others". He is probably right, because if the people have a voice in the government, they have more trust in it.

See also //
47 Plutocracy, see p.98

3/ Hack: Democracy means "rule by the people".

No.42
Monarchy Supreme ruler

1/Helicopter View: Monarchy, a form of government in which a single family rules from generation to generation, was the most common form of government in Europe from the Roman era until the end of the 18th century. A combination of republicanism and Enlightenment thinking, which included the idea of individual rights and self-determination, undermined the claims of the monarchs. As a result, many were replaced by republican governments, although some survived as constitutional monarchies, in which power was devolved to other, more democratic, bodies of government. Today there are 12 monarchies left in Europe, including the elective monarchy of the Vatican City as well as those in Belgium, Denmark, Norway, Spain, Sweden and the UK, plus various principalities and the Grand Duchy of Luxembourg. In all, there are 43 countries around the world that still have a monarch as head of state.

Queen Elizabeth II and her family (below); Edward VII; Henry VIII; Ibn Saud; Sobhuza II of Swaziland and his son Mswati III (opposite).

2/Shortcut: In a traditional monarchy, power is invested in one person, the monarch – normally a king or queen, but sometimes a prince or princess, an emperor or empress – who holds the position until death or abdication. The monarch usually takes power through hereditary succession. There are also examples of monarchs invoking religious justification for their position, claiming they have been chosen by God. European history is littered with power struggles between monarch, nobility and their subjects. Some monarchs, such as Henry VIII and Louis XVI, were absolute monarchs with total power and did virtually anything they wished. Today, the only remaining absolute monarchs are said to be found in the Middle East, in particular in Saudi Arabia, although the Sultan of Brunei in Asia wields tremendous power through oil wealth and as a representative of a ruling family that has been in power since the 15th century, and King Mswati III of Swaziland in Africa is famous for his lavish lifestyle and retains power by appointing many of the country's Members of Parliament. Britain's Queen Elizabeth II is the longest-reigning and oldest monarch in history. While she is largely a figurehead with no political power, she is also the head of state of 15 other nations.

See also //

16 The Federalist Papers, p.36

56 Separation of Powers, p.116

83 The US Constitution, p.170

3/Hack: Monarchy is a type of government ruled by a single person.

No.43
Presidential The real head

![Helicopter icon] **1/ Helicopter View:** A presidential system is one in which the chief executive (the President), who is elected by the people for a fixed term, is the head of the government *and* the head of state. The system was invented by America's Founding Fathers in 1789 as an alternative to the parliamentary system. In the presidential system, all three branches of government – executive, legislative and judiciary – are separated from each other by the terms of the Constitution, which grants the President extensive powers: in domestic and foreign policy, over the economy and the armed forces, and as ceremonial head of state. In one of the Federalist Papers, statesman Alexander Hamilton (1757–1804) wrote: "Energy in the executive is a leading character in the definition of good government. It is essential to the protection of the community against foreign attacks: it is not less essential to the steady administration of the laws…[and] to the security of liberty". Although the President dominates the executive, responsibility for policy is shared with Congress and the Supreme Court, each of which can block a Bill at any stage of its passage. Congress, which comprises the House of Representatives and the Senate, is the legislative branch of government, while the judicial branch, which interprets and applies the law, is made up of the Supreme Court, interstate and district courts. Other democracies, such as Argentina, Brazil, Mexico and the Philippines, follow the same model as the US.

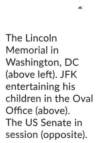

The Lincoln Memorial in Washington, DC (above left). JFK entertaining his children in the Oval Office (above). The US Senate in session (opposite).

2/Shortcut: Supporters of the presidential system say it is truly democratic because the President is directly elected by the people, and that a fixed term of office ensures stability. They also argue that the checks and balances of the separation of powers ensure the quality of legislation, enhance limited government and protect individual and minority rights. Critics point out that the individual power of the President can degenerate into dictatorship, a problem that could be compounded as it is difficult to remove a president mid-term. There is also the danger of political gridlock if the majority party in the legislature is from a different party to the President.

See also //

16 The Federalist Papers, p.36

56 The Separation of Powers, p.116

60 The Electoral College, p.114

83 The US Constitution, p.170

84 The Bill of Rights, p.172

 3/Hack: A presidential system of government is one in which the president is the chief executive and is elected directly by the people.

No.44
Parliamentary
Collective responsibility

 1/Helicopter View: The parliamentary system is a popular form of government in which the political party that wins most seats in the legislature (or parliament), as the result of an election, forms the government. The majority party then chooses a leader, normally the chancellor or prime minister, who appoints senior colleagues to his or her cabinet (who together make up the executive). The party in second place forms the opposition, whose job it is to challenge the party in power. If there is no majority, then a coalition government made up of a number of parties will be formed by agreement. The winning party will remain in power for a fixed term after which another election will take place. Countries using this system include Canada, Great Britain, Italy, Japan and Germany. Parliamentary government is so-called because the system vests all power in parliament. Often countries with such a system will also have a head of state, who is a ceremonial figure and, aside from signing legislation into law, rarely gets involved in politics. Parliamentary governments normally conduct the legislative function through a one-chamber or two-chamber parliament made up of members accountable to the people they represent.

The Houses of Parliament in London (above); (opposite from left) The Reichstag in Berlin; the interior of the Italian Parliament Building in Rome; the National Diet Building in Tokyo.

2/Shortcut: The main attraction of the parliamentary system is that it is easy to pass legislation, as the ruling party enjoys majority support in the legislature. It also has transparency, in that all issues are discussed in the legislature through questions and answers. As members of the legislature, ministers have to respond to issues raised by other members, some of which have been broached by their constituents. In this way, government is influenced by public opinion. Critics see the system as a form of cabinet dictatorship, supported by majority voting. They also point out that a fixed-term system does not allow for long-term policies. Some question a system that allows ministers, who must be members of the legislature, to be appointed to posts for which they may not be suitable and for which they will rely on unelected civil servants for advice and guidance.

See also //
41 Democracy, p.86

3/Hack: In a parliamentary system, the primary decisions of a country are made by a parliament: a group of people individually elected by its citizens.

No.45
Republicanism
The "unalienable" right

1/Helicopter View: A republic, like a democracy, uses a representational system in which citizens vote to elect politicians to represent their interests in government. However, while democracy is defined as government of the people, a republic is governed by the laws of a constitution. The constitution protects certain unalienable rights that cannot be taken away, even if the government has been elected by a majority vote. In a "pure" democracy, the majority government can impose its will on the minority. Today, many countries are republics in the sense that they are not monarchies. The first such system of government was the *res publica* or Roman Republic (*c.*509–27 BCE), and it was also the system of choice of the commercially driven city-states of Renaissance Europe. It became a powerful force following the American and French Revolutions during the late 1700s, both movements prompted by revulsion at the bloated and corrupt systems of monarchy that had developed in Britain and France, and driven by the need to find new systems of good government. Once free of British rule, the Founding Fathers of the United States of America set about discussing their choice of government at the Constitutional Convention in Pennsylvania in 1787. They opted for a federation of states with a central federal republican government, in which democratic principles are ensured, a system that is still in place today. In France, *républicanisme* eventually emerged as a form of social contract with each citizen engaged in a direct relationship with the state to ensure the primacy of the "general will" of the people.

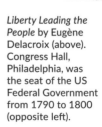

Liberty Leading the People by Eugène Delacroix (above). Congress Hall, Philadelphia, was the seat of the US Federal Government from 1790 to 1800 (opposite left).

2/ Shortcut: Most countries in the world today govern as republics. However, many of them differ in nature. Some operate under a presidential system, such as the USA and France, where the people directly elect a president as head of the government for a limited term. Others use a parliamentary system, in which the people elect a legislature which decides the executive branch. There are also constitutional and parliamentary monarchies that behave as republics despite having royal figureheads.

When the US government moved to Washington, DC in 1800, the Capitol Building (shown below in 1871) was far from finished.

See also //
41 Democracy, p.86

3/ Hack: Republicanism is a political system founded on the rule of law, the rights of individuals and the sovereignty of the people.

No.46
Oligarchy Government of the few

1/Helicopter View: In an oligarchy, a state or society is ruled by an elite few. This could be rule by an aristocracy or some sort of social elite; rule by the clergy, as in a theocracy; or on the basis of technical knowledge and skill, as in a technocracy. Historically, the aristocracy were thought of as the best people to rule because they came from well-respected families and had the benefits of good education. They were usually wealthy and, because of their advantages of status and opportunity, tended to hang on to power. In a theocracy, the elite are religious authorities, priests or ministers, who rule through their interpretation of religious law. A technocracy relies on skills in one or two particular areas of interest, perhaps in finance or law, and is often favoured during times of economic or political crisis. An example is the government formed in Italy in 2011 by economist Mario Monti (b. 1943). He was invited by the Italian president to take the role of prime minister specifically to deal with the country's mounting debt problem and formed a cabinet of unelected financial professionals to advise him.

Below: Louis XIV, known as the Sun King, whose extravagance helped fuel the French Revolution. Opposite: The massive sell-off of large state-owned Russian companies brought great wealth to so-called oligarchs, such as Roman Abramovich (opposite).

2/ Shortcut: In the modern era, the term "oligarch" is mainly associated with individuals, usually businessmen, who became hugely rich on the pickings associated with the break-up of the Communist Soviet Union in 1991. In an effort to move the country toward capitalism, then president Boris Yeltsin (1031–2007) wanted to privatize state-owned companies and raise much-needed cash. A plan called "loans for shares" was hatched by which some of the largest assets – nickel production, oil companies and others – were leased through auctions for money lent by commercial banks to the government. The auctions were rigged, foreign investors were barred from bidding and insiders were able to do informal deals with former USSR officials to win the bids, often for a fraction of the real market values. Those lucky enough to be in the right place with the right amount of money went from being rich to being fabulously wealthy.

See also //
47 Plutocracy, p.98
50 Theocracy, p.104

3/ Hack: Oligarchy implies government by the few.

Plutocracy
Money talks

1/ Helicopter View:

In a plutocracy, a small group of people in a society rule by virtue of their wealth. It is a form of oligarchy. It is also a self-reinforcing system. When a group of affluent people acquires power, they use their wealth to make sure they get more of it. Perhaps as a result of this, the term is usually used in a pejorative sense. First seen in the classical civilizations of Greece and Rome, experts claim that it was the growth of capitalism that allowed plutocracy to develop. Indeed, some critics claim that capitalism inevitably leads to plutocracy; others that it is merely a possible outcome. It seems most likely that although capitalism created opportunities for everyone to make money, it also opened the door to plutocracy, as it did, for example, for the Medici family in 15th- and 16th-century Florence. But the most obvious example of this system was the United States between the end of the Civil War in 1865 and the Great Depression in 1929. During these years, the country was transformed from a rural republic to a leading industrial power, with the formation of hugely influential industrial monopolies in the transport, petroleum, steel and textile industries. With little competition, working conditions and wages remained low. President Theodore Roosevelt (1858–1919) acted to break up the corporations, saying, "we have come to the stage where for our people what was needed was a real democracy; and of all forms of tyranny the least attractive and the most vulgar is the tyranny of mere wealth, the tyranny of a plutocracy."

The Medici family gained power and wealth through commerce and banking.

2/ Shortcut: Today, the question of whether one nation or another is plutocratic is a hot topic. The debate does not only include the regular capitalist countries, like the UK and the USA, but also post-Communist Russia and the emerging economies of China and India. Although most people can see the benefits of economic development, they are concerned by the fact that only a tiny percentage of the already rich actually benefit from the enormous wealth created, and the political power that comes with it.

Roosevelt's (below left) "Square Deal" aimed to solve the problems of labour and corporate activity. John D Rockefeller (below) was the wealthiest American ever.

See also //
46 Oligarchy, p.96

3/ Hack: A plutocracy is a state or society governed by the wealthy.

No.48
Hegemony Unnamed and unseen dominance

1/Helicopter View: Hegemony is the power and control that one state holds over others. This control is usually political, cultural, economic or military. The term comes from ancient Greece, in which the city-state of Sparta was the *hegemon* (leader) of the surrounding city-states through political and military dominance. A more modern example would be Nazi Germany's domination of Western Europe in 1940. Its military campaign led to the annexation of Austria in 1938, followed by the invasions and occupations of Czechoslovakia, Poland, Belgium, the Netherlands, and Luxembourg. By incorporating these countries, Germany became the hegemon of the region. The most notable political hegemony was the British Empire, which at its height during the 18th and 19th centuries controlled approximately a quarter of the world's population and land area, imposing political and educational institutions and a civil service. Commercial exploitation of Britain's colonies also saw the establishment of an economic hegemony thanks to the East India Company, which made huge profits from trade with India and East Asia.

Cultural hegemony, which describes the dominance of one social group or class in a society, is a subtler concept. The theory was popularized by the Italian journalist Antonio Gramsci (1891–1937). As part of his contribution to Marxist theory, he blamed the state for the continuing power of the ruling class through social institutions, such as schools, that expressed an ideology that invisibly encouraged people to consent to the rule of the dominant group in society.

Lord Clive meeting Mir Jaffar before the Battle of Plassey in 1757. Victory helped establish British hegemony in Upper India.

2/Shortcut: In the modern era, the concept of hegemony has for some replaced the building of empires via colonialism. Since the end of the Second World War, the United States has come to dominate world affairs. The home of the United Nations (UN), the World Trade Organization (WTO), the International Monetary Fund (IMF) and the World Bank, the richest nation on earth has the rest of the world in its grip. Since the end of the Cold War and the demise of Russia, the US has had no particular rival for dominance, so it no longer has to fight for it. Instead, its influence comes from using the increasing pace and scope of economic, technological and cultural activities to stay ahead.

In a cartoon from 1899, Uncle Sam teaches the Philippines, Cuba, Puerto Rico and Hawaii about US dominance.

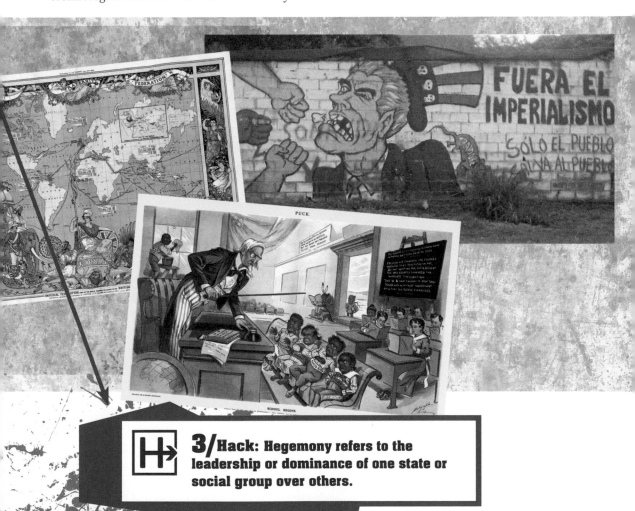

3/Hack: Hegemony refers to the leadership or dominance of one state or social group over others.

No.49
Dictatorship
The cult of personality

Kim Il-Sung // 1912–1994

Kim Jong-il // 1941–2011

1/ Helicopter View: A dictator normally comes to power as the result of a violent struggle, although today it is not unusual to hear about a dictator being elected, most likely through a rigged election. Once in power, a dictator is able to make unilateral decisions without the checks and balances of any other branch of government. A dictator does not rule for the benefit of his nation and its citizens; he does so for himself, his family and his close political allies. Key policies that dictators use to keep their nations' citizens in place include: denying free speech, freedom of religion, a free press and even the freedom to express an opinion that differs from that of the ruler or the ruling party. Another characteristic of a dictatorship is the cult of personality that surrounds the leader. His control of the media enables his supporters to construct a mythology as an all-knowing and benevolent ruler, able to use his wisdom to bring prosperity to the nation. Perhaps the best modern example of this would be in North Korea, where the Kim dynasty has ruled since 1948. It is the foundation on which the edifice of North Korean cultural orthodoxy has been raised.

The Great Dictators of North Korea (above and opposite far right), the Soviet Union and Germany (opposite, from left to right).

2/ Shortcut: The term "dictator" originated in the Roman Republic to describe a magistrate who was granted extraordinary powers in order to deal with a state crisis. However, by the mid-20th century the term became associated with leaders of cruel and oppressive regimes. Joseph Stalin (1878–1953), who became dictator of the Soviet Union in 1929, was responsible for over 30 million deaths as a result of failed policies, executions, famine and war. Adolf Hitler (1889–1945) was the leader of Nazi Germany between 1934 and 1945. His Fascist policies led to the Second World War and the deaths of at least 11 million people, including the mass murder of an estimated six million Jews.

See also //
37 National Socialism, p.78

Joseph Stalin // 1878–1953

Adolf Hitler // 1889–1945

Kim Jong-un // b.1984

3/ Hack: A dictatorship is a form of government in which absolute power is in the hands of one person.

No.50
Theocracy Governing with God's will

1/Helicopter View: In a theocracy, all authority is said to derive from a deity. In practice, it refers to a government operated by religious authorities who claim unlimited power in the name of God. For a state to be a true theocracy, however, its law-makers have to believe that its leaders are governed by the will of God, because its laws are written and enforced based on that belief. In the earliest example, ancient Egypt, the pharaoh was not just God's representative on earth but a god himself (or herself). As a consequence, what he or she said was regarded as law. In some cases, the efficacy of claiming God's will is hard to determine, for example, the government of North Korea. Some regard it as a theocracy because of the supernatural powers attributed to its former leader Kim Jong-il (1941–2011). In the tradition of the Egyptian pharaohs, he was regarded as a living god by his people and worshipped as faithfully as any supernatural deity. In a regime in which there is no room for dissent, the country's state media machine is looking to do the same for his son, Kim Jong-un (b. *c.*1984). A more realistic example of this system is found in Saudi Arabia, which is a theocratic monarchy from the Sunni school of Islam, and one of the most tightly controlled governments in the world. The country has been ruled by members of the House of Saud since 1932. Its constitution is embodied in the Qur'an and its legislation firmly rooted in Shariah law.

Above: The hajj is the annual pilgrimage to Mecca – a journey all Muslims must make at least once. Opposite: Ayatollah Khomeini became Iran's political leader for life in 1979.

2/Shortcut: Iran calls itself a revolutionary theocratic state. It is a recent construct, only established following a revolution in 1979, which deposed the Shah, Mohammed Reza Pahlavi (1919–80), who was well known for his secular activities. A new constitution declared God as the sole head of state and he was embodied by the Ayatollah, his representative on earth. As leader of the revolution, the formerly exiled cleric Ruhollah Khomeini (1902–89) was appointed as head of state to ensure that the people adhered strictly to the principles of Shia Islamic religious practice. Today, Ali Khamenei (b. 1939) runs the country according to traditional Islamic beliefs, albeit assisted by other government officials democratically elected by the people.

See also //

51 Islamic States, p.106

86 Religious Freedom, p.176

93 Shariah Law, p.190

3/Hack: A theocracy is a sovereign state ruled by divine authority.

No.51
Islamic States
The concept of Khilafah

1/ Helicopter View: Islam is a cultural, religious and political system modelled after the rule of Muhammad (c.570–632), the tenets of which are contained in two sacred texts: the Qur'an (the word of God/Allah) and the Sunnah (the sayings of Muhammad, the Prophet). The political system of Islam is based on three principles: Tawheed (Oneness of God), Khilafah (caliphate) and Risalat (prophethood). Tawheed means that God alone is the creator and that an Islamic state's citizens' primary act of faith is to strive to implement His will in both private and public life. An Islamic state's government (caliphate) is primarily based on the application of Shariah (Islamic) law, which is believed to be an extension of God's absolute sovereignty. Its interpretation of the Qur'an and Sunnah, the Risalat (message), provides moral guidance for every action a person takes. In an Islamic state, the leader (or caliph) is obliged by the Qur'an to run the affairs of the people using *shura* (consultation). He is elected based on his competence to lead, not on his policies, because he is required to derive laws based on the sacred texts – and has to implement the laws contained therein, even if they are not convenient. The government must provide full protection for people's rights at all times. In an Islamic state, the leader remains in power until he becomes unjust or incompetent.

In Islam, the purpose of the dress code for men and women is to let them live their lives with modesty, dignity and respect.

2/ Shortcut: Islam is described as a "total way of life", giving advice for all spheres of existence, from individual cleanliness and rules of trade, to the structure and politics of society. It cannot be separated from social, political or economic life, and as a consequence makes no distinction between Church and state. The modern Islamic state is still rooted in Islamic law. However, unlike the caliph-led governments of the past, which were essentially imperial despotisms or monarchies, a modern Islamic state can incorporate modern political institutions such as parliamentary rule, judicial review and popular sovereignty.

See also //

50 Theocracy, p.104
**93 Shariah Law,
p.190**

3/ Hack: An Islamic state is one that insists on the primacy of Shariah law.

No.52
Federalism From little acorns

 **1/Helicopter View:** Federalism is a system of dividing power between a central national government, state government and local government. It has developed particularly in large countries, which have diverse groups of people with different needs but with a common culture that binds them together. The most obvious examples of this system are Canada, Mexico, Brazil, Germany, Australia and the United States. For instance, in America the state of California's requirements, with its 40 million inhabitants, crowded highways and varied climate, contrast with those of the sparsely populated state of Vermont, with its rocky soil and short growing season. While it is obvious that the two states' needs will be different and will require local government to satisfy them, they are both part of America and come under the auspices of the national government. In the United States, the Constitution of 1787 created the federal system by limiting the national government's responsibilities to certain areas, such as creating a currency, regulating commerce, road building, collecting taxes, foreign policy and declaring war. In 1791, the Tenth Amendment gave all the powers not in the original list to the states themselves, including establishing local elections and governments, schools, local trading and public safety. Of course, the division of responsibilities has developed since then.

The Bundesrat in Berlin, home of the advisory body of the Federal Republic of Germany (above). Federalism is a system of government that allows two or more entitles to share control over the same geographic regions (opposite).

2/ Shortcut: The pros and cons of federalism have been the subject of debate since the founding of the United States and continue today. Critics points out the difficulties it causes in the creation of national policies, and that it can often lead to a lack of accountability. It is said that federalism cannot function well when people take little notice of state government; average turnout at local elections in the United States is less than 25 per cent. In contrast, many Americans feel close ties to their home state, and are often more trusting of local officials to take the right decisions for them. The system also encourages pluralism – getting people involved in their government – which leads to political stability.

See also //
53 Autonomy, p.110
54 Local Government, p.112
83 The US Constitution, p.170
84 The Bill of Rights, p.172

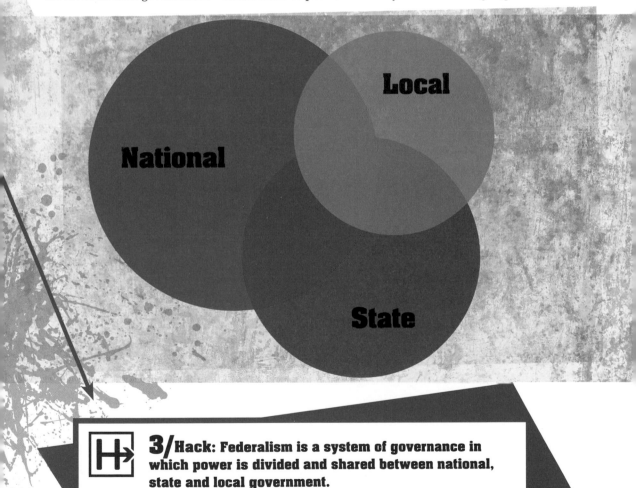

3/ Hack: Federalism is a system of governance in which power is divided and shared between national, state and local government.

No.53
Autonomy Within or without

1/Helicopter View: Autonomy is the capacity and right of a country, or state or region or other jurisdiction, to govern itself. In international law, it might refer to national sovereignty, when a former colony is seeking independence from its colonizers; it could mark the end of monarchical rule or it could be invoked by an ethnic or religious group feeling unrepresented in national government and seeking some form of self-rule. It can also apply to corporations, organizations and local governments. A good example of this can be found in the political arrangements of native peoples living on reservations in the United States. The reservations are ruled by tribal governments, which are responsible for enforcing laws within their borders as they see fit. As well as respecting their own laws, however, the citizens are expected to abide by state and federal laws of the USA. Similarly, US territories like Puerto Rico or Guam have been given a considerable amount of autonomy by the federal government, although they remain part of the United States. Perhaps the most interesting examples are found in struggles for regional autonomy, such as in Spain, where both the Catalan and Basque regions have been granted local control of some functions of government.

In the 19th century, the US government ordered Native Americans off their ancestral lands and on to reservations. In 2017, Cheryl Andrews Maltais (below) of the Wampanoag tribe participated in a Senate Indian Affairs Committee discussion.

110

2/ Shortcut: Both the Catalan and Basque regions of Spain, which have their own languages and culture, have been given a degree of autonomy by the national government over the years and have their own independent parliaments. However, for some this has not been enough. In the Basque country, a campaign of violence waged by the militant group ETA aimed at achieving full independence lasted 40 years and claimed over 800 lives, and only came to an end in 2010. In October 2017, the Catalan government held a referendum on independence from Spain, sparked by the 2008 financial crash and subsequent national public spending cuts. The referendum was declared illegal by Spain's constitutional court. In the event, 90 percent of voters wanted to split from Spain and, although the turnout was only 43 percent, independence was duly declared. The national government immediately dissolved the Catalan parliament and sacked its leaders. The situation remains volatile.

In 2017, the Catalan government declared independence from Spain, but the move was declared illegal, the government dissolved and its leaders, including Carles Puigdemont, arrested.

See also //
52 Federalism p.108
33 Nationalism, p.70

3/ Hack: Autonomy is the right to self-government.

No.54

Local Government
Public service provision

1/ Helicopter View: Almost all nations have a system of local government, which vary in nature enormously across the world. In general, it serves two purposes. The first is the management of local issues and the organization of local services; the second is to involve citizens in determining what services they require. Local government usually takes the form of a public body authorized to administer a limited range of important public policies and services for the cities, towns and local districts they represent. It normally occupies the third or fourth level of the pyramid of governmental institutions, and derives its authority from a regional government, which, in turn, takes its authority from a national level. Its primary function is to deal with issues of local concern, such as road maintenance, street lighting, refuse collection, parks, public amenities and so on, but it might also provide local administration for healthcare and the emergency services. Because it is local in nature, however, the quality and character of a particular local government is determined by a number of different factors: for example, economic resources, political pressures, national and local traditions, bureaucratic professionalism, geography and the social organization and beliefs of the citizens.

Above: New York, like many of the world's major cities, has its own local government and a mayor – Bill de Blasio assumed office in 2014. Opposite: Ken Livingstone was Mayor of London from 2000 to 2008.

2/Shortcut: In cities and large towns, local government is generally political in nature and decidedly bureaucratic. The world's major cities, like London, New York and Kolkata, are represented by elected mayors who wield a considerable amount of political power, are responsible for utilities, transport and housing, and have the budgets to match. While this type of local government is high profile and mostly autonomous, critics point out that it is only really able to fulfil the first of its purposes: that of providing services. In smaller communities, however, local government is likely to be both more effective and more democratic. With an executive made up of elected councillors from the locality, and business often discussed at public meetings, the sense of involvement and level of participation among the population is normally significant, therefore effectively fulfilling local government's second purpose.

See also //

52 Federalism p.108

3/Hack: Local government is an administrative body for a specific geographical area.

No.55
Seats of Government

Symbols of power

1/Helicopter View: Different countries have different forms of government, but the buildings and institutions in which the business takes place are often quite similar. All states have the following ministries (although not always with the same names): interior, foreign affairs, defence, justice and finance. The structures must be able to host the three branches of government: executive, legislative and judiciary, plus a huge number of other government workers. Estimates of those employed by governments can be staggering. For example, according to Citibank figures, in 2011 50 percent of workers in China were employed by the government, although this probably included those working in state-owned enterprises. The figures are more modest in the US and the UK: 15 percent and 20 percent respectively. As landowners, the Russian and Chinese governments are the biggest, with the US Federal government in third place as owner of 308 million hectares (760 million acres). Most governments have a parliamentary building, ministries, law courts, town halls and offices, and those that have been established for a long time may have former royal palaces that can be used for formal state occasions.

The Hungarian Parliament, Budapest (above); (opposite) The Great Hall of the People, Beijing; The Reichstag in Berlin.

114

2/Shortcut: Many government buildings not only play a role in the political life of a country, but are also historical monuments and help project an image of the country's heritage to its citizens and to visitors and tourists. With substantial finances available and frequently motivated by pride and heritage, these buildings are inherently symbolic and often architecturally striking. Among the most beautiful is the Hungarian Parliament, which is situated on the bank of the Danube river in Budapest. The largest and tallest building in the city is one of Europe's oldest legislative buildings. In Berlin, the German Parliament, the Reichstag, was originally built in 1894, but was badly damaged by fire in 1933 when the government was moved to Bonn. It returned to Berlin in 1990 following reunification. In 1999 it was renovated with the addition of a huge glass dome from where the public can watch the administration in action, a symbol of the transparency of today's federal democracy.

3/Hack: Government buildings are often symbolic of the power and authority vested in them.

No.56
The Separation of
Powers In pursuit of liberty

1/Helicopter View: The separation of powers is a system of dividing up political authority so as to ensure that no single branch becomes too powerful. The concept can be traced back to the Greek philosopher Aristotle (384–322 BCE), but the phrase "separation of powers" is credited to Charles-Louis de Secondat, Baron de Montesquieu (1689–1755), an 18th-century French Enlightenment thinker. In 1748 he wrote *The Spirit of the Laws*, a so-called scientific study of government. He described what he thought of as an ideal constitution based on his understanding of the English constitution at that time, identifying the three distinct functions of government: the legislative, the executive and the judicial branches. He asserted that, to most effectively promote liberty, these powers must be separate and acting independently. These ideas were hugely influential during a time of great political change, when memories of the tyrannical governments of the past were still raw. America's Founding Fathers were determined not to make the same mistakes. James Madison (1751–1836) said in one of the Federalist Papers, "The accumulation of all powers, legislative, executive, and judiciary, in the same hands, whether of one, a few, or many… may justly be pronounced the very definition of tyranny." They were similarly important to the victors of the French Revolution of 1789, whose plans for democracy and government were set out in *The Declaration of the Rights of Man*, one of the most important documents in the history of civil rights. It listed the rights of all men, at all times and all places, and included freedom of religion, freedom of speech, freedom of assembly and the separation of powers.

James Madison (above) and John Jay (opposite), argued in favour of the separation of powers in the Federalist Papers.

2/Shortcut: The strongest practical expression of the separation of powers was incorporated into the United States Constitution, drafted in 1787 and enacted in 1789. This constitution clearly divides government into three branches: executive (the President), legislative (Congress) and judicial (the Supreme Court). It also includes a rigorous system of checks and balances so that if one branch exceeds its authority or acts contrary to the national interest, the other branches can block it.

See also //

13 The Spirit of the Laws, p.30

16 The Federalist Papers, p.36

82 The Rights of Man, p.168

83 The US Constitution, p.170

3/Hack: The separation of powers divides governmental responsibility so that no branch becomes too powerful.

No.57
Suffrage The right to vote

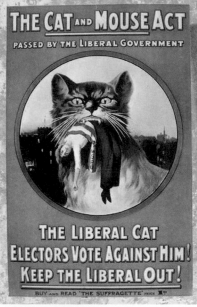

1/ Helicopter View: Suffrage, taken from the Latin *suffragium*, means the right to vote either in electing public officials or in accepting or rejecting proposed legislation, something that has become a cornerstone of the world's democracies. It is now regarded as an unalienable right for all citizens, rather than a privilege, but for millions of people voting has not always been an option. The history of voting and voting rights has been one of gradual extension, from elite groups of well-born, usually wealthy, men, to all citizens over a certain age. It has taken a long time, but in today's democracies it is the system employed to ensure that governments are responsible to those who elect them to govern. Voting, of sorts, has been around since the invention of democracy. In the ancient Greek city-state of Athens men who had done their military training were able to vote on all decisions that affected the city. In England in 1432, Henry VI passed statues declaring who was eligible to vote (male owners of land worth at least 40 shillings, or a freehold property): perhaps half a million souls nationwide. By 1885, changing conditions and attitudes had enfranchised just under 8 million adult males in Britain.

Imprisoned Suffragettes often went on hunger strike and were released as they became ill. Once the women had recovered, the police re-arrested them and returned them to prison.

2/ Shortcut: In the mid-19th century, the campaign for women's suffrage began to gain momentum, particularly in France, Britain and the United States, but in 1893, New Zealand became the first self-governing country to allow women to vote. In Britain and America progress was slower, leading to mass protests, and direct and sometimes violent actions, including arson attacks and even bombings. It was their role in the war effort during the First World War that gave women, particularly in Britain, a new-found political confidence, which was rewarded in 1918 by the Representation of the People Act. The act allowed women over 30 who owned £5 of property, or who had husbands who did, to vote and to stand for election, and many other countries followed suit during the inter-war years.

In the United States, activists such as Alice Paul (main picture below, right) and Doris Stephens (main picture below, second to right) organized street campaigns.

See also //

39 Feminism, p.82
59 Voting Systems, p.122

3/ Hack: Suffrage is the right to vote in political elections.

No.58
The Party System
Political competition

1/Helicopter View: A political party is an organization that represents an ideology or vision from somewhere along the political spectrum, with specific goals usually published in written form. It then seeks to influence government policy by nominating candidates and trying to get them elected to political office. The system in which the parties work normally fits into one of the following three categories: a one-party system, a two-party system or a multi-party system. One-party systems are authoritarian in nature; in such states there are no opposition parties. The Italian Fascist Party and the Nazi Party in Germany were both totalitarian single political parties. Similarly, Communist states, such as Russia and China, have one-party systems. The USA has a two-party system, as do other nations where there are two main parties plus a few other less influential ones, such as the UK, Belgium and Ireland. In this type of system, it is common for power to swing from one party to the other and back again. At certain times, the two main parties may share power in a coalition, which might also be an alliance between one of the main parties and another smaller party. A multi-party system features several equally popular parties and often results in a coalition. France, Italy, Switzerland, Germany, Japan and India are examples of countries with this system, which can lead to political instability, as has been the case in both France and Italy for many years.

The US has a two-party system, China one party. A multi-party system, as in India, often results in a coalition government.

120

2/ Shortcut: Few countries have actually chosen their party system, but instead they have evolved from the political values and even the voting systems of each state. For example, a state with great social, economic, political, cultural, religious and linguistic diversity, like India, needs a multi-party system. In contrast, a state based on an ideology, such as Communism, is bound to have a single-party system, while a theocratic state, founded on a religious creed, will also have a one-party system but one based on the religion of the majority.

See also //
23 The Political Left, p.50
24 The Political Right, p.52
41 Democracy, p.86
59 Voting Systems, p.122

3/ Hack: The party system describes the normal number of parties that compete effectively within a particular state.

No.59
Voting Systems

✗ marks the spot

1/Helicopter View: There are a number of different voting systems employed around the world, which have a variety of features ranging from proportionality of the votes cast, the connections between elected politicians and their constituencies and the extent to which voters can choose between candidates. In the UK, the US, Canada and India, a 'first-past-the-post' system is used. Electors vote for one individual and the candidate with the most votes in each constituency becomes the Member of Parliament (MP) for that seat. All other votes are disregarded. The 'alternative vote' system, as seen in Australia, requires electors to place candidates in order of preference. If no one wins an overall majority, the candidate who received the fewest first-choice votes is eliminated and the second choices of the voters who backed them are allocated to the other candidates. This process continues until one candidate obtains an overall majority. In the 'single transferable vote' system, favoured by Ireland, Malta and Tasmania, voters rank the candidates according to their preference, and each constituency elects between three and five MPs, depending on its size. Those candidates reaching a certain quota of votes are elected. Surplus votes for the elected candidates and the votes for the least-supported candidate are redistributed on the basis of voters' second choices. The process continues until the required number of MPs reaches the necessary quota. The 'additional member' system, used in Germany, combines constituency elections with a directly elected proportional component. Voters cast two votes: one for an MP and one for a party.

Mature democracies, such as India and the UK still rely on traditional systems of casting and counting votes, but new digital systems are being developed.

2/ Shortcut: In many democracies, one system is used to elect general representatives, while another is employed to elect the executive. In France, they favour a 'two-round' system in both presidential and parliamentary elections. Voters go to the polls and pick their favourite candidate. The votes are then counted. If no one gets 50 per cent of the votes, the top two candidates go through to the next round a few weeks later and the one who gets the most votes wins. In the US, the President is elected according to a unique system called the 'electoral college'.

See also //

60 The Electoral College, p.124

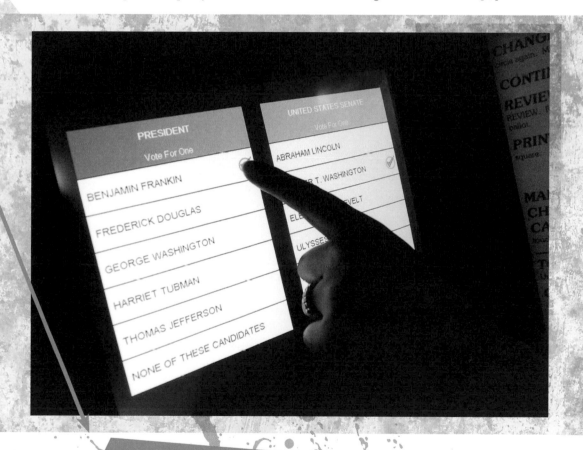

3/ Hack: A voting (or electoral) system is the way we choose our political representatives.

No.60
The Electoral College

270 to win

 1/Helicopter View: The "college" is the process by which the President and Vice President of the United States are elected. The presidential election is held every four years. On the Tuesday after the first Monday in November, voters go to the polls and vote for their choice of President. However, they actually vote for their candidate's electors: usually party loyalists, donors or other key players that the candidate or the candidate's party wants to reward. Every state gets at least three electoral votes (a state's number of electors is the same as the total number of its senators and representatives in Congress, and the minimum is three). As the nation's capital, Washington DC also has three electoral votes. California has the most votes, with 55, then Texas with 38; New York and Florida have 29 apiece. In all but two states (Maine and Nebraska) the candidate who wins the state, regardless of his or her margin of victory, gets all of the electors. By law, these electors gather in their respective state capitals on 19 December for the second stage of the process – officially casting their votes. There are 538 electoral votes in all, so the winning number is 270. The states' governors certify the tally and the number of votes cast are presented to a joint session of Congress on 6 January, with the winner sworn in two weeks later.

The map of the US shows the number of electoral votes assigned to each state. The votes are certified by the states' governors and presented to a joint session of Congress for counting.

2/Shortcut: The electoral college was originally established by the Constitution as a compromise between those who wanted an election by Congress and those who wanted a popular vote. There was concern that even qualified citizens (generally white, male landowners) wouldn't have the information necessary to make a truly informed decision. Generally, electors have voted as they are pledged, although sometimes so-called "faithless electors" have broken ranks, though has never affected the final result of a presidential election. Of more concern to those who oppose the system is that twice in the last 20 years the winning president has lost the popular vote but won the election thanks to the electoral college system.

See also //

50 Voting Systems, p.122

83 The US Constitution, p.170

3/Hack: The electoral college is made up of electors who cast votes to decide the President and Vice President of the United States.

No.61
Lobbying The dark art

1/ Helicopter View: Political lobbying describes any attempt to influence the actions, policies or decisions of elected officials. The term is said to refer to the lobbies of the Houses of Parliament in London where Members of Parliament (MPs) and peers gather before and after debates. At one end of the scale are emails and letters sent to MPs by private individuals regarding local environmental issues or planning applications, for example. At the other end come the oil companies which want looser regulations on offshore drilling and the pharmaceutical corporations which desire stricter intellectual property laws to protect their patents. In truth, the complexity of the legislative process makes lobbying essential to the function of government. Congressmen or MPs and their staff do not have the time to become experts on every single issue of concern to the people they represent. A seasoned lobbyist not only educates elected officials on the issues, but can also advise on drafting legislation. Lobbying encourages people to play an active role in government and it is a fundamental right that citizens "petition the government". However, the fact is that lobbying is big business, often conducted on behalf of other clients, by firms who specialize in it. In the US in 2014, private interests, including charities, social media companies and airlines, spent $3.5 billion on lobbying. The reason? For every dollar spent, the average return was $220 in federal support and tax savings: an unrivalled return on investment.

Lobbying can take the form of a chat between "old friends", as well as that of an organized mass protest.

2/Shortcut: While there are some countries where lobbying does not "officially" take place, in France for example, many governments have taken steps to introduce a register of official lobbyists in an attempt to prevent corruption, but suspicion still hangs over the practice. Critics point to what is known as the "revolving door" process by which lobbying firms will recruit former politicians (who have themselves already benefited from the process) and make use of the contacts they made during their careers. These lobbyists will seek to persuade their former colleagues to enact legislation favourable to their clients by helping with campaign funds, gifts and meals out and by seeking to influence a politician's constituents to demand a change.

3/Hack: Lobbying is any attempt to influence legislative decisions made by a public official.

No.62
NGOs The third sector

1/Helicopter View: An NGO (non-governmental organization) is a non-profit, citizen-based group that functions independently of government. Usually organized on community, national and international levels to serve specific social or political purposes, NGOs are cooperative, rather than commercial, in nature. Some are staffed by volunteers, others by paid employees. The World Bank identifies two types of NGO: operational, which focus on development projects such as improved healthcare; and advocacy, which promote particular causes like human rights. Despite being independent of government, some NGOs, for example the Environmental Protection Agency in America, rely on government grants. Others are funded by private donations, membership subscriptions, grants and the sales of goods and services. In recent years, globalization has prompted a rise in the importance of NGOs. Many underdeveloped nations have been unable to deal with problems themselves and international organizations, such as the World Trade Organization, have been focused on the interests of capitalist enterprises and offered little assistance. In an attempt to redress the balance, NGOs have evolved to emphasize humanitarian crises, developmental aid and environmental issues.

President Nixon proposed setting up the Environmental Protection Agency (EPA) in 1970, a year of environmental action across the United States.

2/ Shortcut: The world's leading NGOs include CARE, Greenpeace, Amnesty International and Oxfam. There are said to be 40,000 international NGOs in operation today, with some nine million others working locally. NGOs are influential because of their expertise and their access to important sources of information. As a result, a significant share of development aid and humanitarian relief is now channelled through such organizations. NGOs have played central roles in global campaigns against slavery, the trade in ivory, whaling, violence toward women, apartheid in South Africa and the proliferation of nuclear weapons. In some cases, however, the sheer number of NGOs as well as their diversity make it difficult for them to develop a coordinated approach to certain problems. Critics say that another factor that tends to limit their effectiveness is their perceived lack of representativeness, in that much of the work is done in underdeveloped countries and most of the leadership is from Europe or North America.

Amnesty International is one of the world's leading NGOs; pictured here is a demonstration in New York against terror and torture around the world.

See also //

65 International Institutions, p.134

3/ Hack: An NGO is a citizen-based association that operates independently of government, usually to deliver resources or serve some social or political purpose.

No.63
Foreign Policy On the front line

1/Helicopter View: In the modern globalized world no nation can avoid involvement in the international sphere. Because of this a nation's foreign policy is of paramount importance and is formulated at the highest level, either by the head of government or the foreign minister. The foreign policy of the country we live in affects almost every aspect of our daily lives. Prices of goods, the supply of oil, gas and petrol, taxes and the lives and deaths of our nation's soldiers all depend on how we interact with the rest of the world. For this reason, it is essential that foreign policy is pragmatic, diplomatic, realistic and based on a set of sound principles. The first objective of a foreign policy should be to protect the territorial integrity of the country along with the security of its citizens, both at home and abroad. Secondly, it is essential in the maintenance of links with other members of the international community with a view to promoting a country's national interests. For some, this is likely to involve preserving the status quo by adopting a policy of cooperation with neighbours and trading partners. For others, it means embracing policies that can contribute to greater prosperity in the search for enhanced status. However, sometimes the interests of various countries clash and policies become more aggressive, which can lead to diplomatic rows, sanctions and even conflict.

For much of the late 19th and 20th centuries, American presidents sought to prevent any single country from dominating the world's centres of strategic power. Today's diplomats have to find a way to use political power to maintain their country's international interests and values.

2/Shortcut: Almost all nations determine the course of their foreign policies within the limits of their strengths and the realities of their external environment. These factors will include the country's history, size, culture, geography, natural resources and political influence. As well as these internal factors, countries have to consider external factors, such as the rulings of international organizations, like the United Nations (UN) and the World Trade Organization (WTO), and international law and treaties while formulating their policies. It is incumbent on a nation's citizens to hold their leaders accountable for its foreign policy.

See also //
64 Defence and National Security, p.132
65 International Institutions, p.134
92, International Law, p.188

3/Hack: A foreign policy is a set of political goals that outlines how one particular country will interact with others.

No.64
Defence and National
Security
Deflecting threat

1/Helicopter View: A country's defence policy is closely tied to its foreign policy, as protecting sovereign territory is one of its main objectives. In the years after the Second World War, fears of another global conflict were held in check by a system of nuclear deterrents in which the world's two superpowers – Russia and the United States – built up massive nuclear arsenals that were capable of delivering what became known as "mutually assured destruction" (MAD). The idea managed to create a strategic stalemate. There have also been a number of treaties aimed at limiting the destructive capabilities of nuclear weapons, such as SALT (Strategic Arms Limitation Talks) and START (Strategic Arms Reduction Treaty), but many countries are unwilling to abandon them, particularly as other smaller nations are developing nuclear capabilities of their own. MAD did not prevent conflict altogether, and during that period a number of countries were involved in smaller wars using conventional weapons. In recent years, the development of modern weaponry has changed the nature of conflict completely. Powerful missiles can be launched with pinpoint accuracy from thousands of miles away. Because of this the role of international politics and diplomacy has become more and more important. Of similar importance, particularly since the events of 9/11, is national security and the protection of citizens against the threat of terrorism.

The Pentagon is the headquarters of the US Department of Defense, including all three military services.

2/ Shortcut: Since 9/11, a new theatre of conflict has developed, based on conflicting ideologies and multiracial communities and influenced by current technology and communication. This has led to a security dilemma, known as the "spiral model", which has heightened tensions in many parts of the world. As one country increases its security, others respond with similar moves. Some states project an image of strength, which is interpreted by others as aggression. Governments may go further and put restrictions in place on civil and political rights, such as border restrictions, to further maintain security. In turn, these infringements on democratic freedom can lead to unrest and possibly terrorism. At the forefront of the fight against this, governments are increasingly turning to intelligence, surveillance and international cooperation to build an effective defence.

The US national security team gather in the White House's situation room to monitor the progress of the operation to kill Osama bin Laden in May 2011.

See also //

40 Terrorism, p.84

63 Foreign Policy, p.130

66 Realpolitik, p.136

3/ Hack: National security is the ability of a state to cater for the protection and defence of its citizens.

No.65
International Institutions
Global governance

1/Helicopter View: The accepted view is that international institutions are those responsible for the promotion of peace, prosperity and development, whether by economic, social, legal or political means, and that they should always act in the interests of the international community. The formation of such organizations gathered pace in the years after the Second World War, prompted by universal calls for an end to global conflict. Three key institutions were founded in the mid-1940s, the World Bank, the International Monetary Fund (IMF) and the United Nations (UN). Initially, the World Bank and the IMF were involved in the rebuilding of European countries, but during the 1960s they turned their attention to providing loans for African countries and others in the developing world. The UN, which replaced the defunct League of Nations, was dedicated to maintaining international peace and security, developing relationships between nations, better living standards and human rights. It currently has 192 member states, each of which has a vote in its decisions. One of its key achievements was the publication of the Universal Declaration of Human Rights in 1948, which lays out the rights of individuals and still provides a basis for international law on the matter. Today, the UN is deeply involved in setting the international development agenda. Another key player in this sphere is the World Trade Organization (WTO), set up in 1995 to oversee the "rules of trade" between its 148 member states, specifically by reducing international trade barriers and promoting free trade.

The UN does not have its own military force; it depends on contributions from member states, like this soldier from Canada.

2/ Shortcut: Despite their laudable aims, international institutions such as the UN, the World Bank, the IMF, and the WTO are not without their critics. The financial institutions have been accused of promoting economic systems that do not suit developing nations, often increasing poverty and leaving countries with unsustainable debt burdens. There have also been complaints about inequalities in their voting and decision-making systems. US and European members hold the majority of the voting rights and have been accused of protecting their own interests at the expense of others.

The UN Security Council has five permanent members (China, France, Russia, the UK and the US) and 10 non-permanent member nations elected for two-year terms.

See also //
62 NGOs, p.128

3/ Hack: International institutions are in place to preserve peace and promote security, prosperity and justice throughout the world.

No.66
Realpolitik The art of the possible

1/ Helicopter View: *Realpolitik* is a German word meaning "practical politics". It was first coined by journalist and politician Ludwig von Rochau (1810–73) in his book on the 1848 revolution in Germany. Basically, realpolitik is the idea that in politics compromise is often necessary, and that pragmatism, rather than ideology (idealpolitik), should be the guiding force of a nation's political policies. The German chancellor Otto von Bismarck (1815–98), who once said, "politics is the art of the possible, the attainable, the art of the next best", used realpolitik to great effect in achieving the reunification of the German nation-state in 1871. Since then this practical approach to achieving political objectives has been credited with many notable successes, particularly in the 1970s: for example, US President Richard Nixon (1913–94) opening up Communist China to the West, and US statesman Henry Kissinger (b. 1923) withdrawing American troops from Vietnam by persuading everyone of the pointlessness of the conflict.

Above: Otto von Bismarck. Top: Gerald Ford, Leonid Brezhnev and Henry Kissinger at the SALT talks in Vladivostok, 1974.

2/Shortcut: Realpolitik remains distinct from ideological politics in that it is not dictated by a fixed set of rules, but instead tends to be goal-oriented, limited only by practicalities, a useful tool in the armoury of politicians faced with many of today's complex issues. But some see realpolitik in a different light, criticizing it on a number of levels. Firstly, that it is short term. Good examples of this can be found in the support offered by America to Saddam Hussein (1937–2006) in his war with Iran at the beginning of the 1980s, a move that eventually came at the cost of the Gulf War; similarly, the arming of the Mujahideen to fight the Russians in Afghanistan in the mid-1980s, which ultimately led to the formation of Al-Qaida and the 9/11 attacks. Secondly, that the term is often used to excuse a shameful compromise, such as the modern business deals made with China and Saudi Arabia, despite the appalling human rights records of those countries.

In the 1980s, Ronald Reagan pledged millions of dollars to the Mujahideen for their fight against the Russians, who had invaded Afghanistan in 1979.

See also //
40 Terrorism, p.84

3/Hack: Realpolitik is political policy based on practical objectives rather than ideals.

No.67
Code of Hammurabi
Conduct and justice

1/Helicopter View: Hammurabi (*c.*1810–1750 BCE) was the ruler of Babylon, now in modern-day Iraq. An ambitious warrior king, by 1755 BCE his kingdom included almost the whole of Mesopotamia. With so many lands and cities under his control, each with its own social structure, historians suggest that he was prompted to develop a system of universal laws to apply to all citizens in his newly established empire. Although it is not the earliest system of laws on record, the Code of Hammurabi, which included statutes from its predecessors, remains the most complete written code from ancient times and has served as a model for establishing justice in other future cultures. The 282 laws were originally carved into a black basalt pillar that was 2.4m (8 feet) high and shaped to look like an index finger, obviously for public display. This pre-Biblical code does not set out a complete set of laws; instead it covers specific subjects, such as slavery, financial regulations, marriage and criminal law, addressing circumstances in which offences might take place and prescribing the varying degrees of punishment, compensation for particular injuries, as well as fees for surgeons, barbers and vets. Punishments for lesser crimes often took the form of retaliatory justice following the precept of "an eye for an eye". Capital crimes and other far less serious offences were usually punished by a grisly death. Significantly, the code was gender-biased and distinguished between punishments for the wealthy or noble, lower-class persons or commoners and slaves.

Stele were placed in public locations throughout the kingdom, ensuring that anyone who was literate could read the code and see how the laws applied to them.

2/Shortcut: Despite the draconian nature of many of the laws of the Code of Hammurabi, presumably intended to counter the contemporary feuds and rivalries that existed in that society, others were quite progressive, particularly those concerning divorce and property rights. However, most striking were early incarnations of two laws still in use today: the notion of being innocent until proven guilty and the provision of a minimum wage. The pillar itself, known as a stele, was rediscovered in 1901 by a team of French archaeologists in the ancient city of Susa, in Iran. It is now on display at the Musée du Louvre, in Paris.

Some claim that Hammurabi had a hand in constructing the fabled Tower of Babel, here painted by Pieter Brueghel the Elder in 1563.

See also //

94 Fitting the Punishment to the Crime, p.192

3/Hack: The Code of Hammurabi is the best preserved and most comprehensive list of ancient laws in existence.

The Cyrus Cylinder

Birth of statecraft

Hormuzd Rassam // 1826–1910

I/Helicopter View: There is no doubt that the Cyrus Cylinder, a 23cm (9in) by 10cm (4in) barrel-shaped cylinder made of baked clay, is of great cultural significance. To those who view its replica in a glass case in the UN headquarters in New York, it is a symbol of tolerance and freedom. To others, such as the Shah of Iran (1919–80) who adopted the cylinder as a political symbol during the 1970s, it is "the first human rights charter in history". Neil MacGregor, the former director of the British Museum in London, where the cylinder now resides, has described it as "the first attempt we know about running a society, a state with different nationalities and faiths – a new kind of statecraft". The cylinder is inscribed with an account of Cyrus, King of Persia (600–530 BCE), and his conquest of Babylon in 539 BCE. The story is significant because of the tolerance shown by the conquering king. Instead of plundering his new lands, he sets the people free, letting them go back to their homes and homelands. He lets them take back the statues and worship their gods in their own temples, things normally confiscated or destroyed by conquering armies. It is a message of peace and multiculturalism, advocating rule by pluralism.

Assyriologist Hormuzd Rassam discovered the Cyrus Cylinder, one of the most famous surviving artifacts of the ancient world, in the ruins of Babylon in March 1879.

2/ Shortcut: The Cyrus Cylinder was discovered in the ruins of Babylon, in Iran, in 1879. Some 2,600 years later, it still unites people from different backgrounds and religions with its message of tolerance. Iranians hold the cylinder in high esteem because of Cyrus's Persian roots; Jewish people celebrate the account, claiming it proves the veracity of the story in the Book of Ezra (in the Jewish Bible) in which King Cyrus permits exiled Jews to return to Jerusalem and rebuild the temple. Thomas Jefferson (1743–1826) was inspired by its ideas of religious tolerance of diverse cultures while writing the United States Constitution. Historians today hold the view that the message on the cylinder reflects a tradition in Mesopotamia that new kings began their reigns by producing a "declaration of reforms", a kind of propaganda used to discredit the old regime and welcome in the new one.

See also //
83 The US Constitution, p.170

3/ Hack: The Cyrus Cylinder is said to be one of the world's first human rights charters.

No.69
The Rosetta Stone
Key to the past

1/Helicopter View: The Rosetta Stone is one of the most important archaeological artefacts in history. The 770-kg (1,700-lb) granite tablet (which is a fragment of a larger stele), covered in undecipherable hieroglyphs, was found in 1799 by Napoléon Bonaparte's soldiers while they were rebuilding a fort in the Egyptian coastal town of Rashid (also called Rosetta). Eventually, linguists were able to translate the inscription and discovered that it consisted of a decree written in three different scripts: ancient Egyptian hieroglyphics, Demotic script and ancient Greek. Scholars were able to translate the Greek quickly but it took 20 years before they realized that the Demotic and hieroglyphic texts were an exact match. In this way, the Rosetta Stone proved to be the linguistic key to deciphering hieroglyphics and therefore probably the single most important conduit of understanding between the modern world and ancient Egypt, unlocking the secrets left behind in the myriad carvings and frescos of the pharaonic era. Historians now believe that the text was written in three languages so that most Egyptians could read it. Ancient Greek was the language of the pharaohs, Demotic was the common script of Egypt, while hieroglyphs were the script of the priests.

Experts inspect the Rosetta stone at the 2nd International Congress of Orientalists in London, 1874 (below, left). A suggested reconstruction of some of the missing Greek text (below).

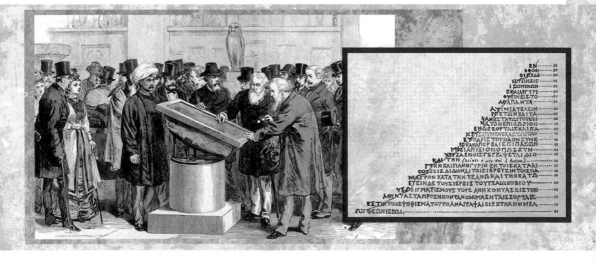

2/ Shortcut: Carved in 196 BCE, the decree on the Rosetta Stone was apparently composed by the priests of Memphis on the first anniversary of the accession of Ptolemy V (*c.*210–181 BCE) to the throne: it celebrated his achievements and announced a series of political and financial concessions that they hoped would maintain his popularity and his hold on political power during a time of increasing restlessness among the Egyptian population. First, it lists the good deeds already done by the young king (he was 12 when he took the throne) on behalf of the temples, thus ensuring the continued support of the priests, then it announces the nullification of debts, a reduction in taxes, the release and pardon of prisoners and rebels and a further increase in benefactions to the temples. Similar stelae would have been placed in temples throughout Egypt promoting the new king's manifesto, although only fragments of the others have been found.

The Rosetta Stone was found in 1899 by French soldiers who were rebuilding an old fort in Egypt.

See also //

1 The Birth of Power Politics, p.6

3/ Hack: The Rosetta Stone is regarded as the earliest example of a political manifesto.

No.70
Magna Carta

The primacy of law

1/Helicopter View: On 15 June 1215, the English King John (1166–1216) met with a number of "rebel" barons at Runnymede on the River Thames near Windsor in the south of England. After years of failed foreign policies, the ex-communication of the king, inglorious defeat at the Battle of Bouvines in France and increasing tax demands to fund another campaign, the barons had rebelled, renouncing their oaths of allegiance to the throne. They accused the king of failing to stick to Henry I's coronation charter against oppression, which sought to bind the monarch to the fair treatment of nobles and church officials, and demanded concessions. The king refused to meet them. However, led by Robert FitzWalter, they gained control of the king's court in London and John had no option but to negotiate. The meeting was significant as it was the first time that a ruling monarch's authority had come into question. The nobles presented him with a list of demands, which

King John signs Magna Carta at Runnymede in June 1215 (below). A rare copy of the first engraved version of the document (opposite).

dealt with specific grievances relating to his rule. He had little choice but to attach the Great Seal and so approve the Charter of Liberties, or Magna Carta, to solve the pressing crisis. However, the settlement did not last long, the charter was annulled and civil war broke out. But a line had been crossed: Magna Carta had set a precedent, establishing for the first time the principle that everybody, including the king, was subject to the law, therefore protecting his people from feudal abuse.

2/Shortcut: In 1225, a substantially rewritten version of Magna Carta was issued by Henry III, of which three clauses remain on the statue books today. One defends the liberties and rights of the English Church, another confirms the liberties and customs of London and other towns, but the most famous is the right of *habeas corpus*, by which all free-men have the right to justice and a fair trial. Over the years, Magna Carta has been highly influential, for example on the Bill of Rights (1791) and the Universal Declaration of Human Rights (1948). Today it remains a cornerstone of the British constitution.

See also //
84 The Bill of Rights, p.172

3/Hack: Magna Carta established the principle that everybody, including the king, was subject to the law.

No.71
The Communist
Manifesto The workers united

1/Helicopter View: In February 1848, a 23-page pamphlet was published in London with little fanfare. It proclaimed that the accomplishments of the Industrial Revolution had transformed the world. New methods of production, communication and distribution had filled the shops with goods, lowered prices and done away with national boundaries. For the first time in history, men and women could see, without illusion, where they stood in relation to others. With the new freedom of trade came great wealth, and here there was a problem, because the wealth was not equally distributed. Ten percent of the population possessed virtually all the property; the other 90 percent owned nothing. As cities and towns industrialized, wealth became more concentrated, and as the rich got richer, the middle class began sinking to the level of the working class. Soon there would be just two types of people in the world: those who owned property and those who worked for them. As ideologies that had once made inequality appear natural and ordained disappeared, continued the text of the pamphlet, it was inevitable that workers everywhere would see the system for what it was,

Marx and Engels (below) predicted uprisings in Europe in 1848 (opposite), as well as today's predatory and polarized capitalism.

and would rise up and overthrow it. The author who made this prediction was Karl Marx (1818–83), and the pamphlet in which he wrote it was the *Communist Manifesto*.

2/Shortcut: If the predicament described in the *Communist Manifesto* seems familiar, then that goes some way to explaining why this slim volume is now the second best-selling book of all time. Marx wrote the text in January 1848, based on a tract written the previous year by his friend Friedrich Engels. Marx also predicted imminent revolution in Europe and the ink had hardly dried on the pamphlets when violence broke out in France in opposition to the banning of Socialist meetings. Revolution spread to many parts of Europe but was quickly suppressed. However, by the time he died, in 1883, Communism had established itself across Europe. In 1917, Vladimir Lenin, a self-proclaimed Marxist, led the world's first successful Communist revolution in Russia.

See also //
21 The Russian Revolution, p.46
27 Communism, p.58
28 Dialectical Materialism, p.60

 3/Hack: The *Communist Manifesto* outlines the beliefs of the Communist Party.

No.72
The Declaration of
Independence Birth of the USA

1/Helicopter View: On 4 July 1776, the Continental Congress, meeting at the Pennsylvania State House in Philadelphia, adopted the Declaration of Independence, officially declaring that the 13 American colonies, then at war with Great Britain, were independent and no longer under British rule. Voting on the document, drafted the previous month by a five-man committee including Thomas Jefferson (1743–1826), John Adams (1735–1826) and Benjamin Franklin (1706–90), had taken place on 2 July, when 12 of the 13 states agreed to independence (with New York abstaining, although it too agreed to it a week later). Amendments were made before its final approval on 4 July – now celebrated as Independence Day. British colonial rule in the Americas had reached its peak by 1750 but relations between the colonies and the mother country began deteriorating in 1763 when parliament demanded more money from the colonists for the right to stay in the British Empire. Armed conflicts between colonists and British soldiers began in April 1775, the Americans then fighting for their rights as subjects of the Crown. Things

changed over the course of the next year, as Britain attempted to crush the rebels by force, and a movement for independence developed. In 1776, a recent British immigrant, Thomas Paine (1737–1809), gave the movement momentum when he published *Common Sense*, arguing that independence was a "natural right"; the pamphlet sold more than 150,000 copies in its first few weeks as the idea turned into reality.

Franklin, Adams and Jefferson (above). On 8 July 1776, the Declaration was read aloud at State House in Philadelphia (opposite).

2/Shortcut: Written mainly by Thomas Jefferson, the Declaration of Independence effectively stated that seeking independence from Britain had become "necessary" for the colonies and outlined a list of grievances against the British Crown. It began with its most famous passage: "We hold these truths to be self-evident; that all men are created equal; that they are endowed by their Creator with certain inalienable rights; that among these are life, liberty and the pursuit of happiness". It also justified the right of revolution on ethical grounds and the right to self-government. With this historic declaration came the formation of the United States of America.

See also //

16 The Federalist Papers, p.36

82 Rights of Man, p.168

83 The US Constitution, p.170

84 The Bill of Rights, p.172

3/Hack: The Declaration of Independence is one of the essential founding documents of the US government.

No.73
The Treaty of Versailles
End of days

1/Helicopter View: The First World War was the most destructive conflict in modern history. With an estimated 18 million dead and 23 million wounded, millions more forced from their homes and catastrophic losses in terms of property and industry, Europe had been brought to its knees when the armistice was signed on 11 November 1918. The formal treaty to end the war was negotiated in Paris during the early months of 1919. Discussions on the terms were held by the heads of government of Britain (David Lloyd George, 1863–1945), France (Georges Clemenceau, 1841–1929), the United States (Woodrow Wilson, 1856–1924) and Italy (Vittorio Orlando, 1860–1952); the Germans were not consulted. The victors of this brutal conflict were in no mood to be charitable and the treaty, presented to the Germans on 7 May 1919, was punitive. Germany had to give up some 15 percent of its European territory and all of its overseas colonies; it had to accept complete responsibility for starting the war and pay for all material damages, maintain only 100,000 soldiers, greatly reduce its naval force and completely abandon its air force. Although angered by the terms offered, the defeated Germans signed the treaty in the Hall of Mirrors at the Palace of Versailles in Paris on 28 June 1919.

David Lloyd George, Vittorio Orlando, Georges Clemenceau and Woodrow Wilson at Versailles, May 1919 (below). The dismantling of German weapons of war began soon after. Today, some historians argue that the treaty's harsh terms contributed to the rise of Hitler (opposite).

2/ Shortcut: The Treaty of Versailles seemed to satisfy the Big Four, who felt it was a just peace after the First World War. Germany was weak enough not to attack France, but strong enough to keep the Communists in the east in check, and the treaty made provision for the League of Nations, which was set up to end warfare throughout the world. However, the treaty left a mood of anger in Germany, particularly because of the war guilt clause and the magnitude of the reparations imposed. Many German citizens felt that they were being punished for the mistakes of their government. Today a number of historians believe that the unjust terms of the treaty represented one of the platforms that gave radical right-wing parties in Germany, including Adolf Hitler's Nazi Party, such credibility with mainstream voters in the 1920s and early 1930s, thus sowing the seeds of the 20th century's second great conflict.

See also //

22 Age of Extremes, p.48

3/ Hack: The Treaty of Versailles marked the formal end of the First World War.

No.74
The Beveridge Report
Slaying the five giants

1/Helicopter View: In 1941, the wartime coalition government under Winston Churchill (1874–1965) began planning ahead for a post-war Britain, and asked the Liberal economist Sir William Beveridge (1879–1963) to write a report on the state of poverty. The snappily titled "Social Insurance and Allied Services" was published on 1 December 1942 and was an instant bestseller. Politicians debated it, journalists wrote about it and the public bought it to read; a summary of the 300-page report sold more than 600,000 copies. The central message of the Beveridge Report, as it was known, was that five giants – want (poverty), disease (health), ignorance (education), squalor (housing) and idleness (employment) – were holding back progress. The solutions put forward included the setting up of a national health service, a welfare system "from the cradle to the grave" for those not in work (24 shillings per week for a single person and 40 shillings for a husband and wife), a family allowance (8 shillings per child) and a state pension, all paid for by affordable monthly payments made by those in work. The report estimated the cost of this service to be £697 million.

Labour's Clement Atlee (opposite) won the 1945 General Election by introducing the welfare state outlined in the 1942 Beveridge Report.

William Beveridge // 1879–1963

2/Shortcut: Although the success of the Beveridge Report was due in part to the scope and detail of its recommendations, which were well received by a public that had endured two years of wartime privations and misery, it also caught the mood of the time. Public optimism had risen with victory in the Battle of El Alamein at the beginning of November 1942, allowing people to believe the end of the war might be in sight. The picture painted by the report of a brighter future with a better (and free) health system, better education, better employment and better benefits that promised a break from the hardships of pre-war Britain fitted the prevailing popular mood. In 1945, the Labour Party led by Clement Attlee (1883–1967) won the general election by promising to tackle Beveridge's five giants. Over the next few years, the report's recommendations were implemented, including an expanded National Insurance scheme and the setting up of the National Health Service, now the cornerstones of the British welfare state.

See also //
78 Welfare, p.160

3/Hack: The Beveridge Report was the blueprint for Britain's post-war welfare state.

No.75
The United Nations
Charter Swords into ploughshares

1/Helicopter View: As the war in Europe gradually drew to a close in the early months of 1945, thoughts began to turn to the kind of peace that would emerge from the burning embers of conflict. On 26 June, delegates from 50 nations met in San Francisco to sign the United Nations (UN) Charter, which set out the organization's goals and purposes in 111 articles. The idea of an international body to maintain peace after the war had been discussed in 1941 when US President Franklin D Roosevelt (1882–1945) met the British Prime Minister Winston Churchill (1874–1965), and conversations continued in the coming years. The major Allied powers – Britain, the US, the USSR and China – all agreed that a new organization was urgently needed to succeed the League of Nations, whose inability to prevent the Second World War had seen a decline in its powers. Following arguments on membership and voting, a compromise was reached at the Yalta Conference in February 1945 and all Allied countries were invited to the UN founding conference in California later that year.

2/ Shortcut: Weary of war, sick of conflict and determined not to make the same mistakes of the peace settlement following the First World War, the Charter laid out the UN's ambitions and the organs through which it would achieve them. Its main aim was to encourage the resolution of international conflicts without war by maintaining worldwide peace and security, developing relations among nations to solve economic, social, cultural and humanitarian problems, and by providing a forum in which to discuss them. As well as "turning swords into ploughshares", a biblical phrase denoting peacemaking, the UN was to promote social progress and better living standards, strengthen international law and advance human rights. It would do this through the Secretariat, the General Assembly, the Security Council, the Economic and Social Council, the International Court of Justice and the Trusteeship Council. Between the San Francisco conference and the Charter's ratification on 24 October, two atomic bombs had been dropped in Japan: a tough call for the permanent members of the now Security Council, which comprised the US, Britain, France, the Soviet Union and China.

The United Nations building in New York City (below). A sculpture entitled "Let Us Beat Our Swords into Ploughshares" stands in the building's North Garden (opposite).

See also //

65 International Institutions, p.134

73 The Treaty of Versailles, p.151

3/ Hack: The UN Charter serves as the constitution of the United Nations.

No.76

"I Have A Dream"
Fight for civil rights

Martin Luther King Jr. // 1929–68

1/Helicopter View: The so-called "I have a dream" speech was delivered to a crowd of some 250,000 people by Martin Luther King Jr (1929–68) from the steps of the Lincoln Memorial in Washington, DC on 28 August 1963. King's appearance was the highlight of the March on Washington, a one-day event protesting against racial discrimination and calling for economic opportunities and the passing of the Civil Rights Act then being discussed in Congress. The huge crowd comprised a great mix of people: black, white, artists, students, ministers, housewives, labourers. It was hot, nearly 32°C (90°F) at midday, and as speaker followed speaker, singers Mahalia Jackson (1911–72) and Bob Dylan (b. 1941) followed Joan Baez (b. 1941) and others, the crowd's attention was wandering. However, all eyes were on King, including those of the national TV networks, when he began speaking. As a young Baptist minister, King had risen to prominence in the late 1950s and early 1960s and was a regular speaker at events organized to publicize the problems of African Americans as they protested against discrimination, segregation and prejudice.

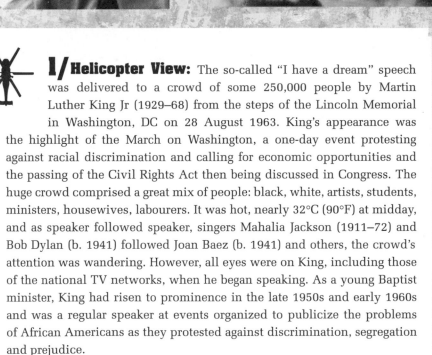

King's speech in Washington, DC in 1963 was influential in Lyndon Johnson signing the Civil Rights into law in 1964 (opposite).

2/Shortcut: Martin Luther King Jr began by speaking about the unfulfilled promise of equality made by the Founding Fathers. Maintaining a positive, uplifting tone, he stressed the need to continue with "the fierce urgency of now", the struggle, through non-violence, toward integration. Then, apparently abandoning his script, he said, "I have a dream…that one day my four little children will live in a nation where they will not be judged by the colour of their skin but by the content of their character…that one day little black boys and black girls will be able to join hands with little white boys and white girls as sisters and brothers." He had used this "dream" theme in speeches before and had been advised not to use it here but those words, beamed across the continent on the news networks that evening, struck a powerful chord. The Civil Rights Act, which ended segregation in public places and banned employment discrimination on the basis of race, colour, religion, sex or national origin, was passed the following year.

See also //

87 From Slavery to Civil Rights, p.178

 3/Hack:Martin Luther King's "dream" speech is regarded as one of the most iconic in American history.

No.77
Tax and Spend
Where your money goes

1/ Helicopter View: A government does not have its own money and requires its citizens to contribute theirs, through taxation, to fund the goods and services it provides. One of the major responsibilities of any government is to determine how much tax should be collected and how the money should be spent. This can be direct tax, on income or wealth; or indirect tax, on transactions, like VAT or sales tax, and on excise, for example on alcohol, tobacco and fuel. A particular government's economic policy is likely to depend on its political ideology: a right of centre government is most likely to ask for less direct tax and therefore reduce public spending; a left-leaning government is happy to ask for more in direct taxation in order to fund greater public expenditure. For most people there seem to be a bewildering number of taxes, which will include, among others, those on income, social security, property, inheritance, wealth, goods and services, licence fees and council taxes. In most developed countries the rich will pay the most tax. In the UK, for example, the top 1 percent of earners pays more than half the total income tax bill. This stands as a warning to governments not to tax the rich too much, as they might leave for countries with more favourable rates.

Deciding how much tax to collect and how to spend the income is one of a government's major responsibilities. The prime consumers of taxes raised are pensioners, health services, the armed forces and education.

2/ Shortcut: The income from taxes is collected by a specialist government department and then handed over to the treasury for distribution. For any particular government, for example in Europe, the biggest outlay is likely to be on pensions and welfare (approximately 25 percent), then health (17 percent) and education (10 percent). There will also probably be significant spending on defence, paying off debts, local government and child benefits/tax credits. The remaining money will be required to fund the activities of various government departments, justice, food and agriculture, transport, science, energy, the environment, international affairs, business innovation and culture/media/sport.

See also //

62 NGOs, p.128

78 Welfare, p.160

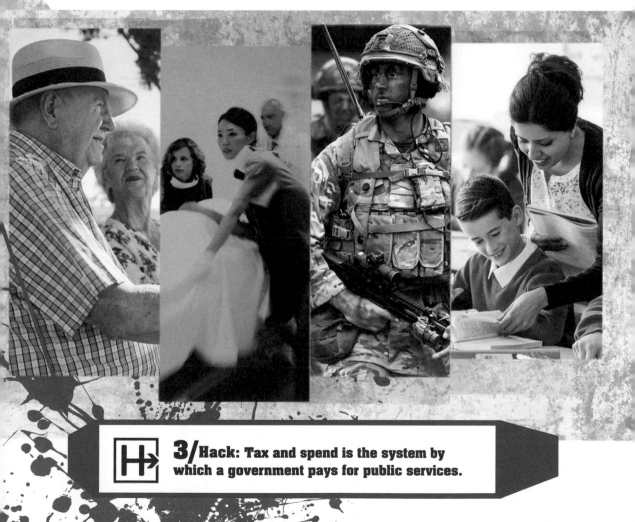

3/ Hack: Tax and spend is the system by which a government pays for public services.

No.78
Welfare
Economic safety net

1/Helicopter View: Although the World Bank has stated that poverty is in decline, the figures remain staggering. In 2013, it announced that 10 percent of the world's population (767 million people) lived below the poverty line, on less than $1.90 per day. One method of combating this is welfare: an economic safety net for veterans and the elderly, those with illness or disability and those with dependent children. In most developed countries, welfare is provided by the government from tax revenue, by NGOs, charities, social groups, religious groups or by inter-governmental organizations. As a concept, welfare is not new. The Roman emperor Trajan was known for his *alimenta*, which provided food, money and subsidized education for orphans and poor children throughout Italy. Historically, the Church has provided for the poor and helpless. In the Islamic world, the government has always collected Zakat (a kind of charity/tax), which is distributed to the poor and needy. In the late 19th and early 20th centuries, various governments started to develop "welfare" programmes, most notably the German Chancellor Otto von Bismarck (1815–98), David Lloyd George (1863–1945) in Britain, who introduced National Insurance in 1911, and US President Franklin D Roosevelt (1882–1945), who developed his New Deal through which money was spent on projects to provide employment during the Great Depression.

Government-run welfare programmes have only been in place since the late 19th century.

160

2/ Shortcut: Today EU countries spend an average 19.5 percent of GDP on welfare and cases of extreme poverty are rare. Naturally, the system has its critics: those that say it is too expensive, that it reduces the incentive to work, that it is paternalistic and that it only offers short-term solutions. But new research in developing countries – like India, China and Nigeria – which have not set up welfare programmes, reveals some stark truths. Despite significant progress in terms of general economic development, these countries are falling behind in their fight against poverty. The Industrial Revolution had dramatic effects on poverty in Britain, the US, Germany, France, Italy and Spain, but these countries managed to eradicate extreme poverty only after the creation of modern welfare states in the years after the Second World War, a fact of which developing economies should take note.

See also //

74 The Beveridge Report, p.152

3/ Hack: Welfare (or "welfare programme") refers to support provided for those unable to support themselves.

No.79
Nationalization/
Privatization   No silver bullet

1/Helicopter View: In the last 60 years or so support for nationalization or privatization has been a stereotypical indicator of where someone stands on the political spectrum, with those on the left supporting nationalization and those on the right in favour of privatization. Supporters of state ownership are particularly keen to see industries that supply basic human needs, such as health, energy, education, transport, the armed forces and the emergency services, as services in which profit should not be a consideration. Those in favour of privatization point out that it creates competition and investment, which leads to improved profitability, productivity and pricing. Naturally, the pendulum of popularity of each system swings as a left-wing government replaces a right-wing government and vice versa. At the end of the Second World War, many European countries chose social democratic governments, because they offered attractive solutions to post-war reconstruction and did so in a way that benefited everyone. Experts recommended nationalization to produce employment, education, health and cultural vitality for all. The pendulum swung in the 1970s as worldwide recession brought an end to post-war recovery. A number of right-wing governments began to identify privatization as a way of raising revenue. In the 1990s the world's governments sold off $25 billion in state-owned enterprises, and that trend has continued. Leaving aside political affiliation the question is, which system works best?

The Privatization v Nationalization debate usually concerns industries that cover basic needs, like energy, health, education and transport.

162

2/ Shortcut: Neither nationalization nor privatization can guarantee success. There are natural monopolies, industries broadly immune to competition, such as the mail service, some transport services, the police and the armed forces, where state ownership seems the most sensible option. And there are examples of successful privatizations of telecoms companies, utilities, energy and railway companies. But neither system is foolproof. Results of privatization schemes have been decidedly mixed. Sometimes productivity has increased dramatically; sometimes investors have skimmed off all the profits. In some cases, performance has improved in the year or two before privatization, suggesting that state-run enterprises can be well run if the political will exists. The fact is that both systems can work given the right conditions.

See also //

**77 Tax and Spend,
p.158**

3/ Hack: Nationalization and privatization describe the process by which assets and/or enterprises are transferred into public and private ownership.

No.80 Globalization

Who does it work for?

1/Helicopter View: The world is becoming increasingly interconnected as a result of massively increased trade and cultural exchanges. The globalization process has been taking place for centuries, but has speeded up over the last 50 years. The key factors have been improvements in transportation, freedom of trade, advances in communications through the internet and social media, and the fact that some countries have cheaper labour along with sufficient skill levels to attract investment. In the longer term, globalization may ultimately reduce the importance of nation states. In recent years, supranational institutions such as the European Union, the World Trade Organization (WTO), the G8 and the International Criminal Court have emerged to facilitate international agreement. Practical effects of the globalization process have been to increase international trade, ensure a reduction in barriers of trade and investment between different economies, the development of multinational corporations, such as McDonalds, Shell, Apple and Starbucks, and a greater dependence among big companies on the global economy.

Globalization has created an international free market that has mainly benefitted large multinational corporations like Starbucks, Apple, McDonalds and Shell (below).

2/Shortcut: The process of globalization has encouraged companies to invest in other countries. For example, many firms are relocating call centres to countries like India, where wage costs are lower. This inward investment benefits developing countries because it creates employment, growth and foreign exchange. Some foreign companies are criticized for exploiting cheap labour, although they frequently offer higher wages than local firms. However, the reality is that businesses in dovoloping countries often find it difficult to compete. Restricted to producing primary products, they face high start-up costs, slow growth and volatile price fluctuations. They may also have to compete with multinationals that are trying to force out local retailers, and struggle to employ skilled workers who have left for better paid jobs in other countries.

Many multinational corporations have taken advantage of cheap local labour, for example, by relocating call centres (below right). In recent years, anti-globalization protests have been held at events such as the G20 summit in Hamburg, 2017 (below left).

3/Hack: Statistical evidence shows that globalization is a process that mostly benefits developed economies and is not closing the gap between the world's poorest countries and the world's richest countries.

No.81
The 99 Percent Movement
Haves and have nots

1/Helicopter View: "We are the 99 percent" has become a worldwide rallying cry for those protesting at the growing economic disparity between ordinary citizens and the super-rich. The slogan, implying that the 99 percent were paying for the mistakes of the 1 percent, was adopted by the Occupy Wall Street protesters in New York City's Zuccotti Park, which began on 17 September 2011. The park is located in the heart of the financial district on Broadway in Lower Manhattan, close to Wall Street, among the institutions and key figures that had played a central role in causing the financial crisis that began in 2007, blamed by many for fostering a more unequal economy in the previous decade. The protesters' accusations of the "1 percent" included irresponsible lending, particularly on sub-prime mortgages that led to huge profits through the creation of a housing bubble, tax dodging, skyrocketing executive salaries, the spending of US$1 million a day on lobbying Congress, asset-stripping and the fact that the stock exchange had, in effect, become a casino with technology-driven high-frequency trading worth US$6.1 trillion per day, and all without accountability. The Occupy Wall Street protests inspired an immediate international response. By 9 October, Occupy protests had taken place or were ongoing in more than 951 cities across 82 countries, and in 600-plus communities in the United States.

What began as a small protest in September 2011 has become a global movement against financial inequality.

2/Shortcut: At the time of the Occupy protests in 2011 people argued over the veracity of the 99 percent/1 percent split, but a report published by the Credit Suisse bank in 2017 stated that the world's richest 1 percent now owns half the world's wealth, a huge increase on the levels at the time of the financial crisis. The financial year 2016–17 saw the creation of 2.3 million new dollar millionaires, taking the global total to 36 million. These millionaires, who account for 0.7 percent of the world's adult population, control 46 percent of total global wealth, a figure that currently stands at US$280 trillion. In contrast, the world's poorest 3.5 billion adults, some 70 percent of the world's working population, have assets of less than US$10,000.

See also //
31 Capitalism p.66

3/Hack: The 99 Percent movement has come to symbolize the growing gap between the super-rich and the rest of the world's population.

No.82
Rights of Man
Revolutionary sense

1/Helicopter View: Thomas Paine's *Rights of Man* was written in response to Edmund Burke's *Reflections on the Revolution in France*, published in 1790, which labelled the Revolution a revolt against the fundamental institutions of Western society. Paine (1737–1809) was outraged and published the first part of his most famous work three months later, in 1791. In it, he defended the

The values of the French Revolution were captured in *The Declaration of the Rights of Man*, published in 1789.

revolutionaries, maintaining that the rights of humans – including liberty, property and security – were natural and did not depend on political charter. He argued that the monarch and his government received their authority only through the agreement of the individuals that comprised the nation, and were therefore duty bound to advance the common good. Failure to do this enabled the people to "fire" such a monarch and his government, as had happened in France. The second part, published a year later, claimed that the social order existed despite government not because of it and that hereditary monarchy was a violation of moral law and therefore unjust. He compared monarchy to democracy and found it vastly inferior in every way. Paine then laid out his ideal conception of a democratic constitution and ended by declaring that the English, had they a democracy, would have free trade, no

corporate monopolies, be able to abolish taxes on the poor and provide a wide array of anti-poverty programmes for the old, the sick, the injured, the youth and veterans.

2/ Shortcut: An Englishman by birth, Thomas Paine settled in America in 1774 and made his name with *Common Sense*, a pamphlet advocating independence for the American colonies. Having enjoyed much freedom of thought in the New World, he returned to England in 1787, where he wrote *Rights of Man* prompted by the crisis in France. For Paine, the French Revolution represented the chance for a new beginning, an age of reason based on natural rights no longer denied by privilege and the past. His book was a massive success, selling more than 100,000 copies in its first three years of publication. A hero to some, Paine was labelled a radical by others and fled to France in 1792. He never returned home.

Thomas Paine wrote *Rights of Man* in 1790, the year after the French Revolution.

See also //

14 A Civil Society, p.32

17 Origins of Conservative Thought, p.38

72 The Declaration of Independence, p.148

3/ Hack: Thomas Paine's *Rights of Man* is one of the great political tracts of history.

No.83
The US Constitution

We the people...

1/ Helicopter View: Following the Declaration of Independence in 1776, the US was governed according to the principles of the Articles of Confederation, a wartime "constitution" adopted by the original states that retained most political power at state level. Critics of this situation, among them George Washington (1732–99), Alexander Hamilton (1757–1804) and James Madison (1751–1836), took advantage of the Constitutional Convention, held in Philadelphia in the summer of 1787, to suggest the creation of a new, more effective constitution. Most of the delegates agreed and discussions began on ideas proposed by Madison, known as the Virginia Plan. These included the primacy of national government, the separation of its executive, legislative and judicial functions, and a bicameral system of Congress. Other plans were presented and discussed, resulting in compromises and revisions. A final draft was prepared with a preamble beginning "We the people…" asserting that the government of the US was for the people, and six articles, including Madison's Virginia Plan, state/government relations, the right to amend the Constitution, the abolition of slavery by 1808 and a statement that the Constitution was to be the supreme law of the land. Although not everyone was satisfied, the document was signed by 39 of the 55 delegates on 17 September and put forward for ratification.

George Washington // 1732–99

2/Shortcut: The ratification process for the US Constitution (nine of the 13 states had to approve the wording for it to become law) began on 28 September 1787 in Congress, by then in New York City. Two parties of opinion soon developed: the Anti-Federalists were opposed to its acceptance, while the Federalists were in favour. Differences centred on the amount of power vested in central government and levels of state representation. Debate raged, fuelled by the publication of the Federalist Papers, which appeared in newspapers in late 1787 in support of ratification. In December, the first five states signed. After a number of compromises and promises of further amendments, other states followed. In June 1788, New Hampshire became the ninth signatory and the Constitution was adopted, becoming law the following March, one month before the inauguration of America's first president, George Washington (1732–99). The US Constitution is the oldest written national constitution in use.

George Washington, former commander in chief of the Revolutionary forces, attended the Constitutional Convention at Independence Hall in Philadelphia (below) in May 1787.

See also //

16 The Federalist Papers, p.36

72 The Declaration of Independence, p.148

84 The Bill of Rights, p.172

3/Hack: The US Constitution defines the principal organs of government and the basic rights of citizens.

No.84

The Bill of Rights

Safeguarding liberty

1/Helicopter View: Several sticking points had developed during the process of the creation of the US Constitution, and a number of compromises were suggested to elicit a favourable decision on ratification. James Madison (1751–1836), by then a member of the newly established House of Representatives, went through the Constitution in the months after ratification to address the issues put forward by its most influential opponents. Of major concern to several states was the lack of constitutional protection of individual liberties and rights, the need for clear limitations on the government's power and a declaration that all powers not delegated to Congress should be reserved for the states themselves. On 7 June 1789, Madison, a Virginian, submitted 12 amendments to Congress with the intention of answering the criticisms of the Anti-Federalists. One of the main critics of the Constitution was Madison's fellow Virginian George Mason (1725–92), who had written the Virginia Declaration of Rights in 1776 and was astonished that the new document did not contain one. Mason was persuaded to sign the 1788 ratification only on the expectation of such an amendment. With the full support of newly elected President George Washington, the house ratified all but two of Madison's suggestions on 15 December 1791 and they became Amendments One to Ten of the Constitution.

The Bill of Rights was intended to provide constitutional protection for individual rights and liberty, mainstays of Americanism today.

172

2/Shortcut: Drawing on a number of different sources, James Madison used his knowledge of several earlier documents, including Mason's Virginia Declaration, Magna Carta (1215) and the English Bill of Rights (1689), which limited the power of the monarch. The amendments to the US Constitution ratified in 1791, known as the Bill of Rights, guaranteed certain basic protections for citizens: freedom of speech, religion and the press; the right to bear and keep arms; the right to peaceably assemble; protection from unreasonable search and seizure; and the right to a speedy and public trial by an impartial jury. For his contributions to the drafting of the Constitution, as well as its ratification, James Madison became known as "Father of the Constitution".

See also //

70 Magna Carta, p.144

83 The US Constitution, p.170

James Madison // 1751–1836

3/Hack:The first ten amendments to the US Constitution make up the US Bill of Rights.

No.85
Freedom of Speech
Limit or no limit?

1/Helicopter View: The concept of free speech has been around since the formation of the Athenian Assembly in the late 5th century BCE, and was upheld during the Roman Republic. Now regarded as a fundamental right of democracy, it is enshrined in the constitutions of many nations. Freedom of speech covers the spoken and written word, art, song and performance, as well as symbolic speech – when an action expresses an idea – such as flag burning. However, some forms of speech are not protected, including obscenity, pornography, plagiarism, libel/slander, hate and speech that causes offence or compromises public security. Proponents of free speech point out the incalculable value of the uninterrupted flow of information and ideas it allows, something amplified many times since the invention of the printing press in the 15th century. Critics saw this as a "menace", likely to assist the spread of sedition and heresy, a train of thought that developed into the idea of censorship, an attitude put firmly in its place by the writer George Orwell (1903–50), who wrote, "If liberty means anything at all, it means the right to tell people what they do not want to hear."

George Orwell said, "If large numbers of people believe in freedom of speech, there will be freedom of speech even if the law forbids it."

FONDATION DE LA RÉPUBLIQUE.

George Orwell // 1903–1950

2/Shortcut: In today's globalized world in which cities contain citizens from every nation and social media carries news and opinion instantaneously, speech has never been freer. In consequence, perhaps, the issue has become a hot topic. While the physical confrontations that arise from the abuse of free speech are dealt with by law, cyberspace has yet to come under effective legal jurisdiction. As a result, there are those who claim the right of "free speech" to spread their unacceptable opinions on race, to recruit terrorists or to criticize feminism, Islam, social justice or political correctness. Some say that this unregulated new medium has to take some blame for the apparent polarization of global political opinions in recent years; others say that it is *because* of this that we need free speech more than ever. After all, even a suspected murderer should have the right to a fair trial.

See also //

86 Religious Freedom, p.176

3/Hack: Freedom of speech is the principle that all human beings have a right to express themselves without facing violence, intimidation or imprisonment.

No.86
Religious Freedom
The moral compass

1/ Helicopter View: Freedom of religion is the right to practise any religion (or no religion) you choose without interference from the government. Historically, many countries had an official religion. Members of the government had to be part of the official Church, often deciding the laws by which the citizens lived. Those who practised a different religion were in danger of persecution. The growing divide between Church and state during the Middle Ages was marked by an increase in religious tolerance. However, it was religious intolerance that caused the Pilgrims to leave England for New England in the early 17th century. Of the settlers that landed in Massachusetts in 1620, 35 were members of the Separatist Church (a radical faction of Puritans), escaping persecution because of their beliefs. Despite this, the new colony did not tolerate any opposing religious views. Indeed one Pilgrim, Roger Williams, was turned out of the colony and founded Rhode Island, the first settlement with no established Church and the first to grant religious freedom to everyone, including Quakers and Jews. This sentiment finally found expression in the First Amendment of the Constitution, part of the Bill of Rights, which insisted on the separation of Church and state and prohibited laws instituting a national religion or impeding the free exercise of religion for its citizens.

Members of the Catholic Christian minority in Pakistan, who have suffered prejudice for their beliefs (above). Jerusalem is held holy by Judaism, Christianity and Islam (opposite left).

2/ Shortcut: Throughout history religion has played a stabilizing role in society. When practised freely, religion is able to establish a moral compass for people to follow, which in turn leads to tolerance of differing views and consideration in civil society. The free expression of religion allows pluralistic religious organizations to exist within modern secular states, and can ease ideological conflicts by transforming volatile societies into models of peaceful coexistence. Despite this, religious freedom is not allowed in some parts of the world, for example Myanmar or North Korea, where religious people have been sent to re-education camps; or China, Eritrea and some Muslim countries, where Shariah law is the only religion permitted.

The pre-Islamic Buddhas of Bamyan, Afghanistan were destroyed by the Taliban.

See also //

9 Church and State, p.22
84 The Bill of Rights, p.172
85 Freedom of Speech, p.174

3/ Hack: Religious freedom is the right to practise whatever religion one chooses.

No.87
From Slavery to Civil Rights
The long road

TO BE SOLD,
On Tuesday the third Day
of August next,
A CARGO
of
NINETY-FOUR
PRIME, HEALTHY
NEGROES,
CONSISTING OF
Thirty-nine MEN, Fifteen BOYS,
Twenty-four WOMEN, and
Sixteen GIRLS.
JUST ARRIVED,
In the Brigantine DEMBIA, Francis Bare, Master, from SIERRA
LEON, by
DAVID & JOHN DEAS.

1/Helicopter View: The journey from slavery to equality for Africans has been long and bitter, nowhere more so than in the United States. The first Africans to arrive at Jamestown, in 1619, were traded as slaves and denied even the most basic human rights. It took more than 200 years for abolitionist sentiments to take hold before President Abraham Lincoln's (1809–65) Emancipation Proclamation of 1863 freed slaves still working in the Confederate states. As an institution slavery was not abolished until the end of the Civil War, in 1865, with the ratification of the Thirteenth Amendment, which the southern states were required to sign in order to rejoin the Union. Further amendments guaranteed citizenship and voting rights. However, "Jim Crow" laws on segregation continued to enforce discrimination, particularly in the south, even though black soldiers played a major role in the global conflicts of the 20th century. Those years saw an increase in the number of black people migrating from the south to find jobs in factories in northern cities, resulting in a flowering of black culture in New York and Chicago. In 1954, a landmark ruling by the Supreme Court declared that state laws creating segregated schools for black and white students were unconstitutional, sparking the modern civil rights movement.

Black soldiers fought in all major American conflicts of the 19th and 20th centuries. Rosa Parks (opposite centre) was one of the civil rights activists who paved the way for the election of Barack Obama in 2009.

2/ Shortcut: The struggle for civil rights and social justice for African Americans took place in the 1950s and 1960s. Through the actions of many, from Rosa Parks (1913–2005) who refused to give up her seat on a bus, to the Little Rock Nine who attended a formerly segregated school despite the efforts of the Arkansas National Guard, and the college students who refused to leave a Woolworth lunch counter in Greensboro, North Carolina, without being served, gains were made. President Dwight D Eisenhower (1890–1969) passed the Civil Rights Act, 1957, to ensure black voting rights. The March on Washington in 1963, marked by Martin Luther King's memorable "I have a dream" speech, hastened the passage of another Civil Rights Act the following year, guaranteeing equal employment for all. And in 1968, days after King's assassination, the Fair Housing Act, which prevented housing discrimination, became the last legislation passed during the civil rights era.

See also //

**76 "I Have A Dream",
p.156**

 3/ Hack: For African Americans, the journey from slavery to legal equality has taken more than 400 years.

No.88
Trades/Labour Unions
Workers unite!

1/Helicopter View: Increasing industrialization across the world during the 18th and 19th centuries changed the working patterns of many people. Workers moved from agriculture and craft to the mills and factories in the cities. Conditions were rarely ideal and with new working practices and larger groups of employees some organization was required to deal with practical matters, such as wages, hours and conditions of employment, resulting in the creation of trades unions, particularly for skilled workers. Disputes between management and employees inevitably followed, which reinforced political affiliations. The 20th century saw a rise in power of industrial unions, which also represented unskilled workers. As a result membership soared and the negotiating power of the unions grew accordingly. Unions tend to work through collective bargaining, negotiating not only wages, but also recruitment, layoffs, promotion, hours, discipline and other matters, and threatening to work to rule or strike if agreement is not reached. Another method of negotiation is through political activism, which led in Great Britain to the formation of the Labour Party in 1900. Due to the inevitability of the class consciousness engendered by these organizations, the relationship between trades unions and Socialism has been a long and generally fruitful one.

2/Shortcut: The strength of the Labour movement is linked with general economic conditions. When employment levels are high and wages rising, membership tends to decline, while at times of recession union activity is likely to pick up. Not surprisingly, union membership peaked during the soaring inflation and mass unemployment of the 1970s, but has been in decline since then. As unions have successfully negotiated, among other things, fairer employment law, workers' rights, improved health and safety standards, fair pay and benefits and anti-discrimination legislation, there are fewer reasons for membership. Besides this, the increasing globalization of the workforce has weakened the tactic of collective bargaining, particularly in industries whose workers can be replaced by a cheaper labour force in a different part of the world.

For over 200 years, trades/labour unions have fought for workers' rights.

3/Hack: Trade or labour unions, representing workers in a particular trade or trades, protect workers' rights, pay and conditions.

No.89
The Right to Protest
Taking on the powerful

1/ Helicopter View: Public protest has existed for as long as there have been governments. Of course, as long as there have been protests against government, there have been rules to restrict them. The dynamic process of the relationship between government and the people has often changed the course of history, making the right to protest one of the most fundamental human rights. It is a right enshrined in constitutions, treaties and charters in many parts of the world, usually as the right to speak freely, to march and to campaign. However, it is not an absolute right: there are limits, and those limits rise and fall depending on the amount of freedom the citizens, as demonstrators, demand and the level of restriction that citizens, as voters, permit the government to impose. A balance must be struck between the demonstrators' right to protest and the property owners, businesses and road users that will be disrupted by their actions. Of key importance to the government are matters of public safety and national security, and in recent years the rise of violent protests and terrorism have resulted in the handing out of new statutory powers to the police. Critics are worried that these have prompted the authorities to apply unnecessarily heavy-handed responses.

Protestors through history: Wat Tyler and the Peasants' Revolt and the Boston Tea Party (below); suffragette Emily Davison and anti-Mubarak demonstrators in Tahrir Square, Cairo. (opposite).

THE DESTRUCTION OF TEA AT BOSTON HARBOR.

2/Shortcut: Public protest is deeply rooted in political culture. In England Magna Carta set an example, as the rebel barons forced King John in 1215 to concede that even the monarch was subject to the law, while Wat Tyler (1341–81) led the Peasants' Revolt against the tyranny of feudalism. In Germany Martin Luther (1483–1546) dared point out the Catholic Church's corrupt practice of selling "salvation" for money, eventually sparking the Protestant Reformation. The American Revolution saw the English thrown out of America and the French Revolution led to monarchs being unseated across Europe. The Luddites helped ensure the rise of the labour movement and the suffragettes secured votes for women. Dictators have fallen, unfair taxes have been overturned and racial discrimination discredited – all showing the progress made because people have had the courage and the right to protest against the powerful.

See also //

18 The The *Ancien Régime*, p.40

19 Pioneering the Women's Movement, p.42

70 Magna Carta, p.144

72 The Declaration of Independence, p.148

 3/Hack: Protests have played an important part in the civil, political, economic, social and cultural life of all societies.

No.90
Radicalism Worlds apart

1/ Helicopter View: In political terms, radicalization, taken from the Latin word *radix* meaning "root", has become something of a media buzzword. Historically, the term refers to a 19th-century movement on the left wing of the political spectrum that urged radical reform, republicanism, redistribution of property and freedom of the press. Today it is used to describe the recruitment of members of ISIS, al-Qaeda, al-Shabaab and other extremist groups. Experts believe that the main source of extreme terrorism in the modern world is the widening gap between those who have the most and those who have the least – probably caused by the rapid development of modern-day technology. In our globalized world, with its lightning-speed communications and sophisticated transportation, the disparity of wealth, education and ways of life are there for all to see. In turn, radical groups, like the Taliban and ISIS, have taken advantage of these technologies, particularly the internet and mobile phones, to spread their message and recruit followers through a process of radicalization. Their targets are often young, disaffected and lacking the necessary education to make decisions for themselves, among whom it is easy to cultivate hatred and hostility toward those who are more fortunate.

ISIS have used modern technology to spread their message, recruiting people such as Mohamed Lahouaiej-Bouhlel, who drove a lorry through a crowd in Nice, France, in 2016, killing 86 people.

184

2/Shortcut: Since 9/11, the response from Western communities to terrorist attacks, the beheading of journalists and aid workers and the presence of bomb-making instructions on the internet has been understandably severe. In 2002, President George W Bush (b. 1946) began a "War on Terror" by establishing a detention camp at Guantánamo Bay in Cuba, where more than 800 terrorists have been detained indefinitely, without trial or rights. Although others do not call it a war, the outrage caused by such attacks remains high, as in the horrified response to the news that "The Beatles", so-nicknamed because of their English accents, complained about being stripped of their English citizenship before their trial for killing and torturing dozens of Western hostages in Iraq and Syria. Other experts, however, believe that outrage and imprisonment are not ways to halt radicalization, and suggest new models of prevention and reintegration for actual and potential terrorists.

The Black Lives Matter movement protests against violence and systematic racism towards African American people, at a time when the US has seen a rise in far-right white supremacist groups.

See also //
40 Terrorism, p.84

3/Hack: Radicalization is the process of persuading someone to a adopt radical position on political, religious or social issues.

No.91
Law-making Setting the rules

1/Helicopter View: There are four different types of law: criminal, civil, common and statutory. Criminal law, covering murder, rape and robbery, is enforced by the police and dealt with by public authorities, while civil law concerns an individual's legal rights and includes unfair actions that are not actually crimes. These issues are handled privately or by privately hired lawyers. Common law is a body of unwritten laws based on precedents established by the courts. Some examples might be trespassing, invasion of privacy or defamation. Common law can influence the decision-making process in novel cases where the outcome cannot be determined based on existing statutes. Statutory laws are written laws, usually enacted by a legislative body, such as parliament and/or the executive branches of government. Proposed Bills will undergo a process of examination and review and require the approval of the legislative chamber or chambers and the head of state to pass into law. Although many of these laws will already be laid down when a government takes office, the passing of additional laws and the amendment of others can be seen as fulfilling its duty toward those who voted it into power.

Symbols of the law: Lady Justice, Old Bailey, London; and Statue of the Authority of Law, United State Supreme Court Building, Washington, DC.

2/ Shortcut: Depending on their particular political philosophy, governments will pass legislation on taxation and expenditure, for example, and will take a more authoritarian or libertarian view toward law-making, particularly in terms of criminal law, in order to create the sort of society they want. These laws will then be put in the hands of other public institutions, such as the police, the judiciary, prisons and the probation service, which will put them into practice. Although these institutions are financed by the government, they are independent by virtue of the separation of powers, which ensures that the government remains subject to the law and not above it. However, government influence in this area remains considerable, in terms of the powers it gives to law enforcement, the length of prison sentences, the size of fines imposed and the attitudes toward rehabilitation of offenders it recommends.

Laws are decided by government and put into practice by the police and the judiciary.

See also //

56 The Separation of Powers, p.116

89 The Right to Protest, p.182

3/ Hack: Law-making is one of the principle functions of government.

No.92
International Law
Finding common ground

1/ Helicopter View: In the era of globalization, relations between states and nations have never been more important. International law is a body of rules that governs the interactions between sovereign states and the rules and duties of citizens of sovereign states toward the citizens of other sovereign states. Historically, there had never been a law-making body for international law, but precedent had built up through accords, charters, treaties and so on. It was only with the setting up of the United Nations in 1945 that anyone was charged with coordinating these efforts to form the basis of the law that now governs relations among nations by settling international disputes by peaceful means. Although it does not enforce a "World Law", the International Court of Justice (the UN's judicial arm) can adjudicate in any disputes when both sides agree to abide by its decisions. Over the years, these disputes have included human rights, disarmament and the protection of the environment.

Battles such as San Romano (above left) were dictated by treaty. By the time of the American Civil War, matters were governed by the Lieber Code, passed in 1863.

2/Shortcut: In 1947, the UN's General Assembly set up the International Law Commission to develop international law. It was composed of members who collectively represented the world's principal legal systems and served as experts in their individual capacities. Since then, they have addressed a wide range of topics relevant to the regulation of issues of relations between states, frequently consulting the Red Cross and the International Court of Justice. Today the UN's General Assembly is the most important forum for matters relating to international law. Treaties that it has adopted relate to genocide, racial discrimination, civil and economic rights, discrimination against women, children's rights, nuclear test bans, the financing of terrorism, disability and the laws of the sea. It has also been able to step in to deal with problems as they develop an international dimension, such as protecting the environment, regulating migrant labour, drug trafficking and terrorism.

The Nuremberg Trials, of former Nazi leaders, were presided over by military tribunal (below left). A piece of the Berlin Wall outside the European Court of Human Rights (below).

See also //

8 The Just War Theory, p.20

65 International Institutions, p.134

3/Hack: International law is a system of treaties and agreements that governs how nations interact with other nations.

No.93
Shariah Law Divine guidance

1/Helicopter View: Shariah refers to the religious law of the Islamic tradition, which is regarded as divine law, and is applied in conjunction with *fiqh*, which refers to its earthly, scholarly interpretations. In this way, some aspects of Shariah overlap with Western notions of law, while others concern living life according to God's will. Shariah comes from a number of sources, including the Qur'an, the Hadith (the sayings of the prophet Muhammad) and the rulings of Islamic scholars. All aspects of a Muslim's life are governed by Shariah. In Arabic, Shariah means "the clear, well-trodden path to water" and presents life as a journey with many paths, one of which is clear and straight: this is the Shariah. It regulates all human actions and divides them into five categories: obligatory, recommended, permitted, disliked or forbidden. Most human actions fall into the permitted category. Traditional Shariah laws are often split into four areas: those covering personal acts of worship, laws relating to commerce, those concerning marriage and divorce, and criminal law.

2/ Shortcut: In the modern era, particularly in non-Muslim countries, Shariah-based criminal law is a mix of traditional law and the law of the particular country. The legal process and recommended punishments have similarly been brought into line. Even in Muslim-majority states, traditional Shariah laws are often retained only in areas of family law. Despite this modernization, the role of Shariah law has become a hotly debated one in Western society, where it is frequently associated with cruelty, terrorism and anti-feminism and condemned as archaic. Attempts to impose Shariah on non-Muslims, in Nigeria and Sudan, for example, has led to violence. Some American states have banned it by statute, even for Muslims. This has brought about calls for greater understanding, as many in the West wonder whether Shariah is compatible with secular government, human rights, freedom of speech and thought, and women's rights.

Twelve of Nigeria's 36 states have Sunni Islam as the dominant religion. These states have Shariah Law for Muslims and conventional law for others.

See also //

51 Islamic States, p.106

3/ Hack: Shariah is a moral, legal and religious code followed by all Muslims.

No.94
Fitting the Punishment to the Crime Just deserts

1/Helicopter View: Criminal law defines both crimes and punishments, which are designed to be proportional to one another. It also refers to a government's power to regulate and punish certain behaviours, which are enacted into law and become crimes. Criminal punishment has to be ordered by government and the law, and must serve as a punishment by inflicting unpleasant consequences. There are two elements to criminal punishment. The first is retribution, based on the biblical notion of "an eye for an eye", a principle feature of the Code of Hammurabi. This suggests that the crime should be investigated, the guilty criminal should be held responsible for his actions and be forced to pay his or her debt to society through a punishment appropriate to the crime. The second element is prevention. This theory is more forward-looking in that its purpose is to punish the criminal in the hope that it prevents other, future crimes. This is known as deterrence and assumes that the threat of punishment outweighs the urge to commit a crime. Of course, this is only effective if the criminal fears the likely punishment.

Louis XVI was guillotined in 1793 (below left); peasant rebel Jäcklein Rohrbach was burnt at the stake in 1525 (below). Death by firing squad was the norm in Mexico in 1916 (opposite).

2/Shortcut: Capital punishment, also known as the death penalty, is the ultimate punishment one can receive from a court of law. Historically, it has been used for those found guilty of crimes against government, as well as murder, treason and other capital crimes. It was often administered in a harsh and cruel manner, such as public hangings. As of 2016, more than 50 countries were identified as still having the death penalty. However, the prevailing type of punishment today is imprisonment, for "life", which usually means 12 to 15 years, for murder and other capital crimes, with determinate terms for serious offenders and fines for minor ones. Despite efforts in many countries to rehabilitate prisoners to lead an honest and normal life on their release, reoffending rates and the prison population remain high. It seems likely that more could be done in this area and in helping offenders deal with their drug/emotional/mental problems, but this can only happen with the political will and the necessary funding.

See also //

67 The Code of Hammurabi, p.138

3/Hack: Retributive justice demands a punishment proportional to the crime committed.

No.95
Politics of Science
The uncertainty principle

1/ Helicopter View: "Science is the pursuit of knowledge, knowledge is power, and power is politics" is how Elizabeth Lopatto, science editor at online magazine *The Verge*, puts it. This is a neat way of explaining how closely science and politics are related in the modern world. The key element here, of course, is money. Most basic scientific research uses government grants, and decisions on what to fund and what not to fund are made by politicians and are therefore political. A good example of this is the tobacco industry, which during the 1950s successfully funded think tanks, lobbying groups and other campaigns to mask the links between cigarettes and lung cancer. In 2001, President George W Bush (b. 1946) halted research using embryonic stem cells, despite its potential for finding cures for spinal cord injuries, arthritis and heart disease, because of "deeply held beliefs", and today the world is locked in an "ideological" battle over the existence of climate change. The fact that politicians think and act based on partisan motives and that priorities change as a result of fixed-term elections have called into question the efficacy of government funding of science.

Chemical company DuPont has a bad record of toxic pollution cover-ups resulting in numerous lawsuits brought by the EPA.

194

2/Shortcut: : On the one hand, the 21st century has already seen astonishing advances in science, such as in stem cell therapy, human genome mapping and the discovery of ice on Mars; on the other there is a growing public perception of mistrust in science. There are a number of competing theories explaining this. Some point to the apparent political bias of governments; others to the increasing number of public–private research partnerships whose research and its results are unlikely to contain information that might hurt the industry partner's profits. Another reason is uncertainty. In the absence of absolute certainties, science relies on probabilities and informed guesses for its results. This uncertainty feeds the growth of scepticism, mistrust and the possible withdrawal of state funding, all easily exploitable by political opponents and those in search of funding for themselves.

Stem cell research is inevitably tied to the politics of abortion, with Republicans against it and Democrats, like former President Obama, in favour.

 3/Hack: Science and politics have a complex relationship influenced by the interconnection between politicians and the people they represent.

No.96
Battle for the Environment
Big problems need big solutions

1/Helicopter View: Awareness of environmental issues is at an all-time high but there is little evidence of a coordinated approach to the problems. Of major concern are climate change, pollution, deforestation, scarcity of water, loss of biodiversity, and soil erosion and degradation. There are many reasons for this lack of action. The first is that environmental deterioration is slow relative to political cycles and so impedes effective responses among governments on shorter timescales. The second is that these are "big" problems and require "big" solutions, which would depend on coordinated, collective action and appropriate international governance. Central to this is the fact that environmental problems do not recognize international borders, so clean air, for example, cannot be achieved with the cooperation of only one country. There are problems too with the emergence of new industrial nations, like Russia, Brazil, China and India, which are producing the highest levels of carbon emissions. Although they do have environmental policies in place, high costs and local corruption render them less effective. But the main issue is that where once environmental issues were regarded as scientific and technological, they are now largely political.

2/ Shortcut: Vested interests, the high costs and a lack of political will continue to play a part in the failure of the world's governments to produce a coordinated global plan to fight the battle for the environment. Of course, there has been progress, for example, the huge success of the German energy sector, which in 2017 produced 85 percent of its electricity from renewable resources. But the reality is that the call for action will have to come from the bottom up; the people will need to demand action from their governments. It is time for individuals to realize, for instance, that while one drive to work has a minimal effect on greenhouse gas emissions, several million car journeys will have an impact large enough to change the earth's entire system. In order to "save the planet" the narrative for environmental action needs to become more compelling.

New York City produces 33 million tons of waste per year, while illegal slash and burn causes pollution in southeast Asia (opposite). Levels of plastic in the world's oceans have reached critical proportions.

See also //

97 Climate Change, p.198

3/ Hack: As long as the lack of international cooperation needed to deal with environmental issues continues, the issues facing the world become ever more pressing.

No.97
Climate Change
Temperature's rising

1/ Helicopter View: The most pressing environmental concern the planet faces today is climate change. Also known as global warming, this refers to the rise in average surface temperatures on earth. The world's leading scientists, including those at the US Environmental Protection Agency (EPA) and the National Aeronautics and Space Administration (NASA), believe that this has been caused primarily by the human use of fossil fuels, such as oil and coal, which releases greenhouse gases – in particular carbon dioxide – into the air, trapping heat in the atmosphere. Agriculture and deforestation also contribute to this process. Although the rise in temperature is small – 0.8°C (1.4°F) over the past century – the effects have been profound, and the rate of its rise is expected to increase rapidly during the next 100 years. As the temperature rises, the polar ice caps melt, and sea levels and ocean temperatures rise. An increase in severe weather leads to flooding, droughts and wildfires, threatening homes, lives, wildlife habitats and, as a consequence, will soon cause soaring food prices.

An increase in extreme weather conditions, such as hurricanes, leads to flooding that threatens people and wildlife alike.

2/ Shortcut: Despite the overwhelming evidence, there are still those who refuse to believe either that climate change is happening or that it has been caused by human activity. The countries in which this belief is most prevalent are the US, the UK and Australia, in part because of the way climate science has been politicized, especially in the news media, within those countries. Another factor is that the fossil fuel industries in those countries are gigantic. In the US, the Koch Brothers, founders of Koch industries (originally a petrochemical company) have given 370 million to climate change denial groups and developed a close relationship with Fox News, run by Roger Ailes (1940–2017), who left the company in 2016, and Rupert Murdoch (b. 1931), both climate change deniers. Using this power and influence, they have convinced people that environmental regulations, rather than being good long-term investments, are job-killers, especially in the fossil fuel industry. This has become a clarion call for conservative voters, thus rendering scientific fact completely useless. In the modern world, however, the last word must go to the economists, who agree that acting to reduce fossil fuel emissions would be far less expensive than dealing with the consequences of not doing so.

Sea ice is melting and mountain glaciers are rapidly retreating, a clear sign that the planet's climate is changing.

See also //

96 Battle for the Environment, p.196

3/ Hack: Climate change is a large-scale, long-term shift in the planet's average temperatures and weather patterns.

No.98
The Green Economy

A vision for the future

 **1/ Helicopter view:** A Green Economy can be thought of as an alternative vision for growth and development. The idea was first mooted in the early 1970s following the publication of scientific studies and widespread eyewitness reports of environmental devastation and climate change. In 2011, the United Nations Environmental Programme (UNEP) defined such an economy as "one that results in improved human well-being and social equity, while significantly reducing environmental risks and ecological scarcities. It is low carbon, resource efficient, and socially inclusive". It is an attempt to develop an economy that aims at reducing environmental risks and ecological scarcities, and one that pursues sustainable development without degrading the environment. It is closely related to ecological economics, but with a more politically applied focus.

Key elements of the Green Economy include renewable energy, such as wind power, and reduced reliance on fossil fuels.

2/ Shortcut: The Green Economy is seen as having seven major sectors: renewable energy, green buildings, clean transportation, water management (including purification and water recycling), waste management (recycling and sustainable packaging), land management (organic agriculture, habitat conservation, reforestation and afforestation) and green markets (carbon trading, etc.). Since the global recession in the early 2000s, many economies are taking a closer look at the broad concepts of the Green Economy. Among those leading the way is South Korea, which has committed to spending 2 percent of its GDP on renewable energy, energy efficiency, clean technology and water. Mexico City has also seen success, reducing toxic air pollution through a series of green initiatives. But the most impressive statistic comes from China, which now invests more than any other country in renewable energy. This growth is driven by a national policy that sees clean energy as a major market in the near future, one in which it wants to gain a competitive edge.

See also //

96 Battle for the Environment, p.196

3/ Hack: A Green Economy is one that supports the harmonious interaction between humans and nature and attempts to meet the needs of both simultaneously.

No.99

Post-Truth Politics
Fake news

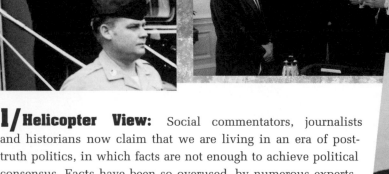

1/Helicopter View: Social commentators, journalists and historians now claim that we are living in an era of post-truth politics, in which facts are not enough to achieve political consensus. Facts have been so overused, by numerous experts, many of them hired for the purpose and using a variety of different sources and statistics, that people no longer find them useful. Prime examples of this came in 2016 when the vast majority of economic, political and business experts said that the facts showed that Britain should remain in the EU, but voters said leave. Similarly, commentators, journalists and political experts said that the facts indicated that Hillary Clinton (b. 1947) should be President of the US, but the voters chose Donald Trump (b.1946). In this new era, fake news has become king. Whether the "story" that EU membership cost Britain £350 million per week, or the "factual" statements Trump made during his campaign, 70 percent of which the PolitiFact website declared to be "mostly false", "false" or "untrue", brought about these results is hard to argue. But they probably helped and this "blurring of the lines" is how fake news works. It is a bit like the sensational but ultimately untrue tabloid headline that passes into folklore despite the apology published a few days later, hidden in the small print on page 15.

The term "post-truth" was first used in 1992, in the context of political scandals like Watergate in 1972 (above left) and the Iran-Contra affair (above) of 1985.

202

2/ Shortcut: It would be easy to form a conspiracy theory based on the use of fake news, but the reality is more prosaic. Fake news stories are popular, like lurid tabloid headlines, and websites and media outlets are able to use them to attract viewers to their sites to generate revenue. Political organizations quickly noted that these stories provided competition for legitimate news stories from established media outlets, spreading confusion and undermining their credibility. The BuzzFeed website reported that the top 20 fake US election news stories received greater engagement from Facebook than the top 20 election stories from major media outlets. Ironically, in an era where there is more information, facts, statistics and data than ever, sifting through the arguments is becoming increasingly difficult.

Since his inauguration in 2017, President Trump has behaved as if arguing from the point of view of objective reality is unnecessary, provoking protests such as the Women's March.

See also //

100 Politics and Social Media, p.204

3/ Hack: Post-truth is the public burial of "objective facts" by an avalanche of media that "appeals to emotion and personal belief".

No.100
Politics and Social Media
The new frontier

 1/ Helicopter View: Whether we like it or not, social media now plays a big part in political campaigns, elections and the way people think about the issues of the day. This new system of communication is particularly relevant during the run-up to an election. The use of sites like Facebook, Twitter and YouTube has made politicians and their parties more accessible to voters; in return, the politicians have instant access to millions of people. Politicians and parties can create and broadcast their political messages, using analytics to tailor-make their points to like-minded voters, at almost no cost. They can also raise funds, advertise campaign meetings, receive feedback, gauge public opinion to refine their policies and raise their profile among younger voters who are impressed by their use of new media. Because of these factors, it is no accident that you might notice how relevant political messages are to you personally. Of course, this takes place 24 hours a day, as do the polls, many of which are now conducted online. One of the most positive aspects of social media is political inclusion, in that voters can more easily interact directly with candidates by attending virtual events and live streaming.

It is claimed that Barack Obama was the first major beneficiary of the influence of social media on politics. A few years later, Facebook, Twitter and other platforms played key roles in the election of Donald Trump.

204

2/Shortcut: The impact of social media on politics is not all positive; rather, it has made the distinction between actual news and fake news more difficult to establish. As well as the official party sites and the recognized news outlets, there are some sites that post false stories deliberately made to look "real", while others post clickbait stories in order to make money and, of course, there are also sites set up to push a particular political agenda or an unsubstantiated conspiracy theory. Another issue is the "bubble" theory, in which analytics influence what you read online, creating the illusion that everybody thinks like you do. Analysts believe this makes people more opinionated and less tolerant of others. Social media's effect on politics is relatively new but its impact is impressive: it has already become politics' new frontier. It seems only a matter of time before internet voting is established, online polling is commonplace and social media is even more influential.

See also //

99 Post-truth Politics, p.202

3/Hack: As social media becomes more popular, its impact on politics will increase.

Index

Picture credits

Alamy Stock Photo age fotostock 154r; American Photo Archive 68; Ammentorp Photography 159l; Art Collection 2 5cl, 42; Art Collection 3 126; B Christopher 158r; Beth Dixson 84; BJ Warnick/Newscom 110r; Chris Hellier 26ar; Chronicle 174l, 180l; classicpaintings 27l; ColourNews 181l; Commercial Megapress Collection 183c; Craig Ruttle 167r; David Cole 5ca; Dino Fracchia 83l; dpa picture alliance 120-121c; es/Benoit Regent/PhotoAlto 159cl; Everett Collection Historical 121b,175l; Everett Collection Historical 204; Everett Collection Inc. 160l; FALKENSTEINFOTO 27r; Frans Lemmens 163l; Fredrick Kippe 159r; Friedrich Stark 176, 191; GL Archive 12r; Glasshouse Images 18; Granger Historical Picture Archive 38r, 44l, 52, 77r, 88, 119l, 119ar; Heritage Image Partnership Ltd. 188l; Historical Images Archive 100; Hi-Story 33l; Homer Sykes Archive 187l; IanDagnall Computing 145c; IndiaPicture 181r; INTERFOTO 20a, 180r; JL Images 155; Josse Christophel 30l, 35l; karenfoleyphotography 124l; Karim Mostafa 183r; Keystone Pictures USA 127; Kristoffer Tripplaar 5r; Lebrecht Music & Arts 146l; Lee Snider 129; Liu Xiaoyang 9l; Lou-Foto 54; Matthew Horwood 122r; Matthias Oesterle 111r; mauritius images GmbH 107; Mike Abrahams 187r; North Wind Picture Archives 149, 178cl; NurPhoto.com 175r; Paul Fearn 122l; PetaPix 63l; Peter Horree 169ar; Pictorial Press Ltd. 32l, 147r, 152; PS-I 165r; RichardBaker 125; Salas Archive Photos 59l; Sean Pavone 177l; Splash News 195l; SPUTNIK 59c, 97r; Stuart Burford 158cr; Tetra Images 158cl; The Artchives 171; The History Collection 13; The Picture Art Collection 22, 26l; thislife pictures 43r; Trinity Mirror/Mirrorpix 113; US Army Photo 159cr; Vladimir Zharikov 97l; World History Archive 32c; World History Archive 32r, 61; Yola Watrucka 158l; Zoonar GmbH/XIAO_MING 11; Zuma Press 106, 123. **Dreamstime.com** Adisa 162; Amanda Lewis 186l; Chaloemwut Phayachueaphetr 8r; Clobigot 81l; Dmytro Shestakov 200; García Juan 6l; Luisa Vallon Fumi 56r; Neil Harrison 6r; Raul Garcia Herrera 7; Rudi1976 25l. **Getty Images** DEA Picture Library 44r; Francis G. Mayer/Corbis/VCG via Getty Images 172; Museum of London/Heritage Images 118r; Topical Press Agency/Stringer 82l. **iStock** artisteer 67r; Cesar Okada 53; diegograndi 66r; kiankhoon 10; omersukrugoksu 56l; strigaroman 16l. **Kiddle Encyclopedia** Adam Smith for Kids (CC BY-SA 3.0) 29ar. **Library of Congress** 4a, 47r, 51r, 64r, 65l, 69l, 73r, 83r, 95r, 98r, 99c, 101, 103cl, 112bl, 115r, 119br, 156br, 178r, 43l, 148l, 173l, Don Halasy 85l. **Metropolitan Museum of Art** Gift of John Stewart Kennedy, 1897 39. **NASA** 201l; Goddard Space Flight Center 85; Jeff Schmaltz, LANCE/EOSDIS Rapid Response 198. **National Gallery of Art Washington** Andrew W. Mellon Collection 36l' Gift (Partial and Promised) of the Jay Family 117. **REX Shutterstock** Associated Press 70l. **Shutterstock** 2p2play 164c; Joseph Sohm 164br; Marco Aprile 165l; Stockforlife 164l; tvamvakinos 164ar; welcomia 201r. **US Department of Defense** U.S. Army photo by Staff Sgt. Christopher Allison 86. **Wellcome Collection** 153r. **Wikimedia Commons** 94, 105; Ali Mansuri (CC BY-SA 2.5) 104; Amada44 89r; Andreas Weith (CC BY-SA 4.0) 199l; Andrew Shiva (CC BY-SA 4.0) 114; Annette Bernhardt (CC BY-SA 2.0) 185r; Anthony Crider (CC BY 2.0) 185l; Arndís Þórarinsdóttir (CC BY-SA 3.0) 57; Blue House (Republic of Korea) 103r; British Government 153l; Bundesarchiv, Bild 102-04062A (CC BY-SA 3.0) 70r, Bundesarchiv, Bild 146-1972-081-03 (CC-BY-SA-3.0) 151l; Bundesarchiv, Bild 146-2005-0076/Scheck (CC BY-SA 3.0) 179l; Bundesarchiv, Bild 183-1987-0922-500 (CC-BY-SA 3.0) 151r; Bundesarchiv, Bild 183-H1216-0500-002 (CC-BY-SA 3.0) 103cr; By Neptuul (CC BY-SA 3.0) 154l; Carl Montgomery (CC BY 2.0) 177r; Cecil Stoughton, White House Press Office 157; Cecil W. Stoughton/NARA 90r; Cezary Piwowarski (CC BY-SA 3.0) 93l; Chateau de Versailles 96; Classical Numismatic Group, Inc. http://www.cngcoins.com (CC BY-SA 2.5) 88-89; Commodore Records 179cb; Courtesy of Granger Collection 130l; Courtesy of the University of Texas Libraries, The University of Texas at Austin 64l; Courtesy Ronald Reagan Library/White House Photo Office 202ar; Daderot 186r; David Plas Photographer (CC BY 2.0) 65cr; Deutsche Fotothek, (CC BY-SA 3.0) 21r; Diorit (CC BY-SA 3.0) 196b; DoD photo by Master Sgt. Ken Hammond, U.S. Air Force 132a; DoD photo by Sgt. Jason Krwczyk, USA 132b; Edward N. Jackson (US Army Signal Corps) 150r; Elroy Serrao (CC BY-SA 2.0) 167l; Environmental Protection Agency 194b; Erik Cleves Kristensen (CC SA-BY 2.0) 101r; francois (CC BY 2.0) 189r; Fyodor Borisov (CC BY-SA 3.0) 163r; Geographicus Rare Antique Maps 14r, 29l, 72-73c; GlacierNPS (CC BY 2.0) 199r; Illustrated London News 1892/Melton Prior 87l; Ingfbruno 67l; J. S. Pughe/Puck Magazine 130r; Jastrow 14l; John Fitzgerald Kennedy Library 58r; John Shandy 164-165; Kacperg333 (CC BY-SA 3.0) 143; Lawrence Jackson/Whitehouse.gov 91; Leepower (CC BY-SA 3.0) 166; Leon Weber (CC BY-SA 3.0) 90l; Library and Archives Canada 60r; Lipton Sale (CC BY-SA 3.0) 95bg; London Stereoscopic Company 45r; © Marie-Lan Nguyen (CC BY 2.5) 12l; Màrius Montón (CC BY-SA 3.0) 111l; Mbzt (CC BY 3.0) 138l, 138r; Mike Gimelfarb 92; Mobilus In Mobili (CC BY-SA 3.0) 203l; MS Cott. Claud DII, folio 116, British Library 145r; National Archives, courtesy of USHMM Photo Archives 188; Nils Ally (CC BY 3.0) 197r; Norman B. Leventhal Map Center, Boston Public Library 101l; Núria (CC BY-SA 2.0) 71; Peace Palace Library/D-Vorm VOF 178l; Photo by Elcobbola (CC BY-SA 3.0) 87r; Pierre-Selim Huard (CC BY-SA 4.0) 108; Portrait of Mao Zedong at Tiananmen Gate by Zhang Zhenshi. (CC BY-SA 2.0) 103l; Presidenza della Repubblica 93ar; Prioryman (CC BY-SA 3.0) 141; Public Domain 4b, 5ar, 5cb, 5b, 9r, 17, 19, 20b, 21l, 23l, 23r, 24l, 24r, 25r, 26br, 28l, 28ar, 28br, 29c, 29br, 30c, 31r, 34l, 34r, 36r, 37, 38l, 40, 41, 45l, 46l, 46r, 47l, 48r, 49l, 50l, 55, 58l, 58c, 59r, 60, 64cl, 64cr, 70c, 72, 73c, 74-75c, 75r, 76l, 76c, 77l, 78, 79, 82, 82r, 85, 89l, 89cl, 89c, 98 inset, 98l, 99r, 118l, 118c, 134-135c, 139, 140l, 140r, 140-141c, 142l, 142r, 144, 146ar, 147l, 150l, 156ar, 168l, 169br, 170, 174r, 178cr, 182l, 182r, 183l, 184l, 188r, 190l, 190r, 192l, 192r, 193, Rama (CC BY-SA 2.0) 35r; Rasiel Suarez (CC BY-SA 3.0) 145l; Richard M. Nixon Presidential Library, Yorba Linda, CA/U.S. Government 128l; Robert Scifo (CC BY-SA 4.0) 161l; Ronald Reagan Library/Michael Evans 137; Simtropolitan 112a; Sindicato Professionales Bellas Artes, U.G.T. 76r; Taipei: National Palace Museum 8l; The National Archives UK Open Government Licence v1.0 (OGL) 89cr; The office of Public Advocate for the City of New York (CC BY-SA 2.0) 112r; The White House Historical Association 116, 173c; The White House Historical Association (White House Collection) 95l, 99l; Thomas Fanghaenel (CC BY-SA 3.0) 115l; TIMEA (CC BY 2.5) 143r; U.S. Department of State 131r; U.S. Food and Drug Administration 195r; U.S. Government 62, 65cl, 81r; U.S. Government 202al; U.S. National Archives and Records Administration 31l, 33r, 36c, 48l, 49r, 51l, 69r, 110l, 124r, 128r, 136a, 156al, 170-171c, 173r, 194a, 196-197c, 202br; U.S. Navy photo: Chief Mass Communication Specialist Steve Johnson 161, Mass Communication Specialist 1st Class David A. Frech 134, Photographer's Mate 2nd Class Jim Watson 63r; UNESCO/A Lezine 177c; US Embassy France 131l; Vlad Lazarenko (CC BY-SA 3.0) 66l; Voice of America 121a; Voice of America News 184r; Walters Art Museum (CC BY-SA 3.0) 136b; White House 203r; White House/Pete Souza 133, 135, 179r; White House/Shealah Craighead 65r; wiii (CC BY-SA 3.0) 93br; www.marxists.org GFDL, http://www.gnu.org/copyleft/fdl.html, (CC-BY-SA-3.0) 146br; yeowatzup (CC BY-SA 2.0) 102. **www.iconspng.com** 16r.